# Macchi C.205 Veltro

## Walk Around®

### Maurizio Di Terlizzi

**English translation by Richard J. Caruana**

Squadron Signal
Publications

Covers by Don Greer
Profiles by Gian Piero Pino and Richard J. Caruana
Line Illustrations by Matheu Spraggins

# Introduction

As Allied bomber raids against Italian cities increased, the Italian High Command issued specifications for a competition as early as 1942 to choose fighters in what would become known as the 'Serie 5' (fifth series). Proposals had to have the aircraft powered by the German Daimler-Benz DB.605 engine, armed with a 20 mm cannon, and named after Canes Venatici In Dante Alighieri's *The Divine Comedy*. Engineer Mario Castoldi, Macchi's brilliant designer, lost no time in redeveling the new fighter by providing his Macchi C.202 fighter with an extensive upgrade. The last two production C.202s of the IX Series were earmarked to become prototypes for the new fighter. The planes were fitted with the new engine, dual oil barrel-type coolers, a retractable tail wheel, and basic armament, which consisted of the standard pair of 12.7 mm guns housed in the forward fuselage and a pair of 7.7 mm guns in the wings. The armament set the standard for all the examples produced in the first series, but the weaponry proved to be inadequate. Fighters from the first production batch, assigned to the 1º Stormo, were already in action during November 1942 in the Sicilian channel. The Italian fighters proved to be on a par with the British Spitfires. A number of versions were produced, including those fitted with a cine-camera at the wing's leading edge and those fitted with underwing pylons to carry external fuel tanks. Eventually, some C.205s housed a planometric photographic camera aft of the pilot's cockpit. A new C.205 version appeared in spring of 1943, and it was armed with a 20 mm. cannon in the wings. These III Series Veltro versions possessed adequate firepower to go up against American B-17s. With the political and military collapse of September 1943, an entire German Gruppe of JG 77 was re-equipped with this Italian fighter. Notwithstanding considerable differences when compared to German fighters, the Veltro was well received. The Repubblica Sociale Italiana was set up in northern Italy in autumn and was equipped with two operational gruppi. The Iº Gruppo, commanded by Maggiore Visconti, was furnished with III Series fighters and a few VI Series. During the numerous dramatic battles in northern Italy, the unit scored a number of victories although it suffered continuous and serious losses of men and machines. In the south, pilots were equipped with a mixed bag of C.202s and C.205s that were recovered from wherever they could be found and repaired as best as possible. With the end of war in Italy, the Veltro's career continued. Several planes remained in service at flying schools while others were sent to the battle between Egypt, which acquired Castoldi's fighter, and Israel. The Veltro's retirement came during the first half of the 1950s. Three Veltros survive today, one of which was restored to flying condition and participated in numerous aerial displays until the end of 1986.

## About the Walk Around/On Deck Series

The Walk Around/On Deck series is about the details of specific military equipment using color and black-and-white archival photographs and photographs of in-service, preserved, and restored equipment. "Walk Around" titles are devoted to aircraft and military vehicles, while "On Deck" titles are devoted to warships. They are picture books of 80 pages, focusing on operational equipment, not one-off or experimental subjects.

## Military/Combat Photographs and Snapshots

If you have any photos of aircraft, armor, soldiers, or ships of any nation, particularly wartime snapshots, please share them with us and help make Squadron/Signal's books all the more interesting and complete in the future. Any photograph sent to us will be copied and returned. Electronic images are preferred. The donor will be fully credited for any photos used. Please send them to:

**Squadron/Signal Publications**
**1115 Crowley Drive**
**Carrollton, TX 75006-1312 U.S.A.**
**www.SquadronSignalPublications.com**

## Acknowledgments

Gabriele Brancaccio, Marco Bovesecco, Phil Butler, Capatti family, Pierluigi Castellani, Sabrina Cavalcanti, Ferdinando D'Amico, Maurizio Delle Site, Gianni Fracella, Franchini family, Marco Gueli, Luigi Iacomino, Vincent Kertmorgant, Roberto Imperi, Paolo Liberati, Ken Lawrence, Maurizio Longoni, Mazzoleni family, Giovanni Massimello, Mauro Morsoletto, Marco Pantoni, Marco Picchio, Valerio Pompili, Alessandro Ragatzu, Rino Righi, Marco Rossi, Andrew Thomas, Riccardo Udiente, Gabriele Valentini, Stato Maggiore Aeronautica Militare, Italian Air Force Museum Vigna di Valle (Roma), AleniaAermacchi, 4° Stormo C.I. All photos by Author unless otherwise credited

**(Front Cover)** 7 Sept. 1943—Sergente Maggiore Laiolo, of the 310th Squadriglia Caccia Aerofotografica, flies at 33,000 feet in his camera-equipped C.205/RF Veltro over Tunis bay to spot and take pictures of enemy activity.

**(Back Cover)** 1 Nov. 1943—Tenente Teresio Martinoli shoots down his last enemy plane over Podgoritza, Yugoslavia, after a crude dogfight with Bf.109s escorting Ju.52s. Martinoli was the 4° Stormo's Ace with 22 individual confirmed victories.

Built at the Macchi plant during the summer of 1943, MM.92215 is a III Series aircraft. Characteristics of this C.205 version include the tall radio antenna, the 20 mm cannon, and the Veltro logo on the fin. The camouflage scheme dates to the end of July 1943, following the deposition of Mussolini and when all aeronautical firms were ordered to remove all regime markings. In fact, there is no trace either of the round fasces marking on the fuselage or within the Saubaudo emblem on the rudder. Only black rings are carried above and below the wings, devoid of fasces. The Regia Aeronautica did not received this machine. It remained at the Macchi works where it was captured by the Germans, who pressed it into service with JG 77. This fighter was lost at Lonate Pozzolo on 28 July 1943, and caused the death of its pilot, Uffz. Soldermann. (Aermacchi)

1° Stormo's badge

4° Stormo's badge
X° Gruppo

4° Stormo's badge
IX° Gruppo

3

Macchi reconfigured this ex-C.202 X series, built by Breda, into a Macchi C.205 Veltro, MM.9546, on 3 December 1949, for export to Egypt. Following the Israeli secret service's dissuasive attempt against the Aermacchi plant, Italy re-acquired part of the consignment headed for Egypt. As a result, this plane example survives today in the Italian Air Force Museum in Vigna di Valle at Rome.

The preserved Macchi C.205 Veltro retains the finish applied by the 4° RMV at Grosseto in February 1994. This paint design replaced the previous erroneous color.

## 51° Stormo's Badge

The third C.205 still in existence is C.205, MM.91818. This plane was converted into a Veltro by Macchi in March 1949 for export to Egypt. On the Veltro's return to Italy, it served with the Lecce Flying School before it was donated to a school at Udine. The plane was maintained in perfect condition by students at that school until it was handed over to Aermacchi and restored to flying condition in 1980. Flown as I-MCVE, the plane was reconditioned after a serious accident and was presented to the National Museum of Science and Technology of Milan in Regia Aeronautica markings. The plane still resides at the museum today. (M. Longoni)

C.205. MM.92166, is the only true Veltro (built as a Veltro, not converted to one) still in existence. In fact, notwithstanding the fixed tail wheel and the post-war style antenna, this plane is fitted with the III Series wings that house the Mauser machine guns. This Veltro was produced in June 1943 and was assigned to the Regia Aeronautica the following month. The plane saw combat with the 378ᵃ Squadriglia (51° Stormo) at Sardinia where it bore code 378-2. This plane shot down a Curtiss P-40 on 22 July and had a second shared victory. Later, the plane destroyed a B-26 Marauder and was hit in combat. After the Armistice, the Veltro served throughout the War of Liberation and eventually with the newborn Italian Air Force. Though the plane was scheduled for Egyptian export, it was returned to Italy before its transfer and ended up at the National Museum of Science and Technology in Milan. Toward the end of the 1980s, Aermacchi bought this plane and preserved it at Venegono Superiore. (Varese)

This first Veltro prototype has a uniform Verde Oliva Scuro 2 upper surface finish and Grigio Azzurro Chiaro 1 undersides. The older C.202 serial number (MM.9287) has been replaced by MM.9847. (D'Amico e Valentini collection)

Toward the end of 1942, Macchi's Veltro production line was in full swing. The plane's complex wing structure gave the C.205 its extraordinary strength.

## Mc.205 Veltro III/VI Series Specifications

| | |
|---|---|
| **Powerplant** | Daimler Benz DB-605 A (Fiat RA 1050 RC 58 Monsone) 12 cylinders liquid-cooled inline engine |
| **Horsepower** | 1,475 hp at takeoff |
| **Armament** | Two 20 mm MG 151 cannons Two Breda SAFAT 12, 7 mm machine guns |
| **Maximum Speed** | 646 km/hr |
| **Wing Span** | 10,580 meters |
| **Length** | 8,850 meters |

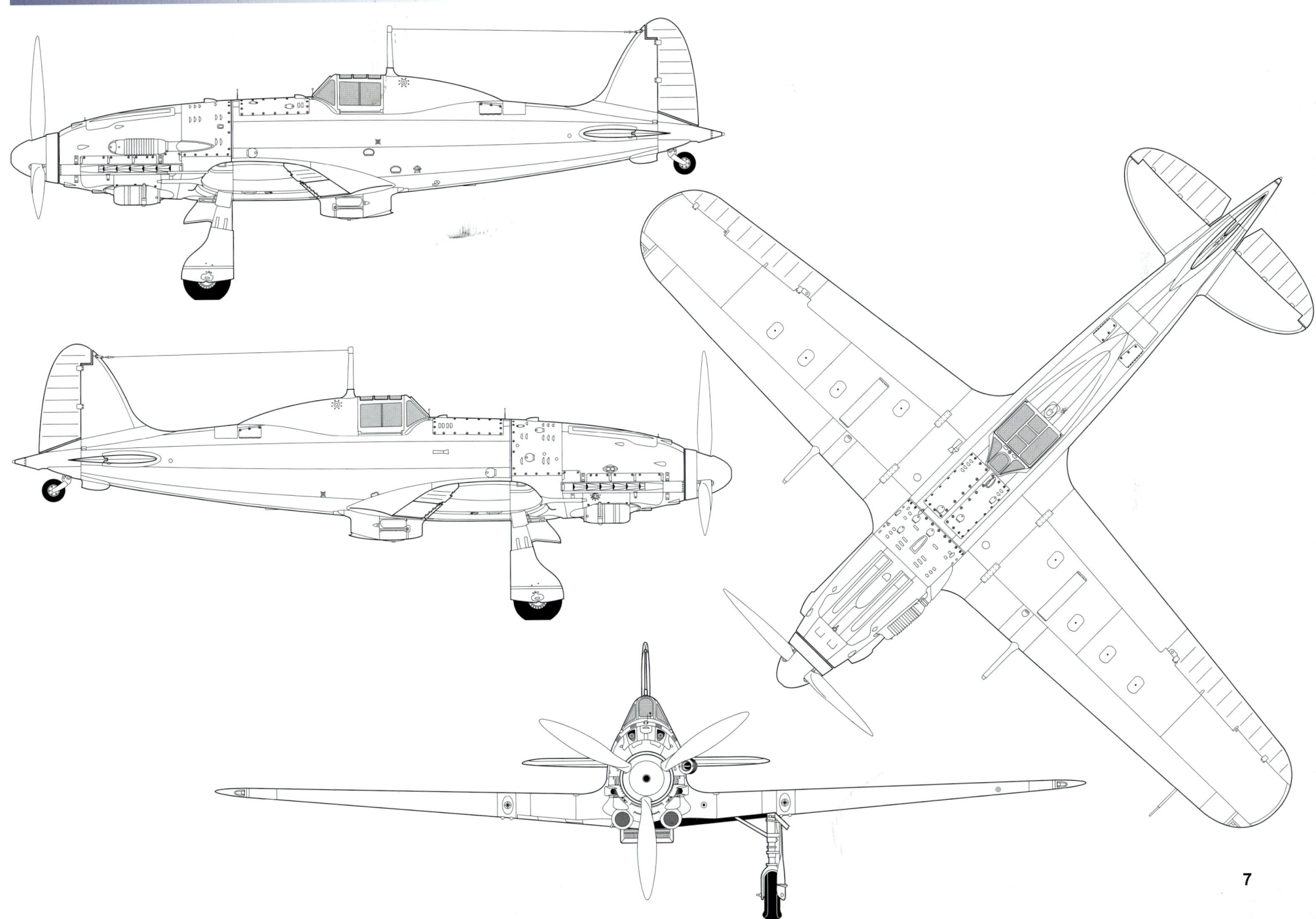

This close-up of the nose detail shows the engine exhaust fairings. Above the fairing are the access panels to the engine's spark plugs and their cooling ducts.

This panel, located below the windscreen, gives instructions for using the synchronization mechanism for the two SAFAT machine guns on the C.205's nose so that the guns did not shoot off the propeller while firing. This mechanism severely handicapped the guns' firing rate.

This metal panel, located below the pilot's cockpit, gives the ground crew a final check reminder to make sure the canopy is closed before the plane takes off.

The 270-liter capacity fuel tank is filled through the C.205's main fuel tank tap. This tank tap also allowed the ground crew to fill the pair of 40-liter tanks located in the plane's wing roots.

The Veltro's nose featured a complicated array of cooling intakes, which were necessary because the engine's temperature tended to rise.

The oval outlet was a combined exit for two tubes. Air used to cool the fuel filters exited the left side, and air from the port 12.7 mm gun's cooling pipes exited the right side.

This small hole at the wing root of the port wing is often confused as being part of the installed camera gun. Actually, this hole supplies cool air to two Ducati-produced fuel filters located inside the main undercarriage bay. Once the air, provided by an aluminum tube, cooled the filters, the air exited through an oval outlet (shown in top right photograph) on the port side of the central nose fairing.

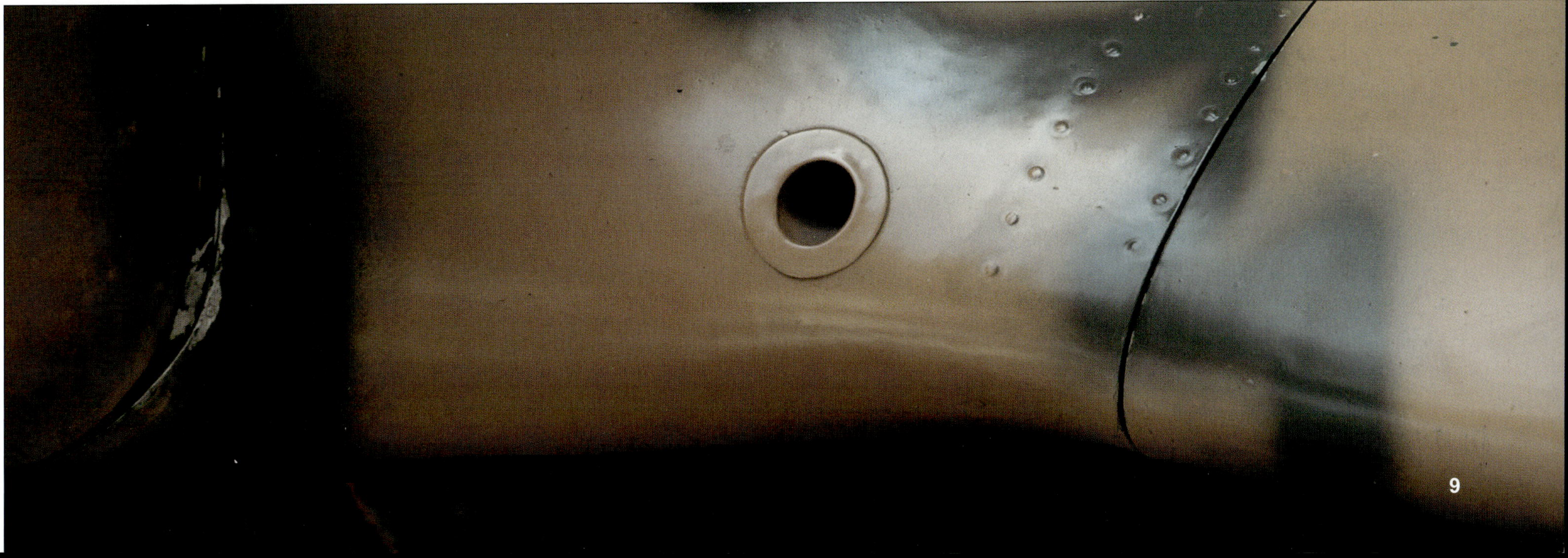

A number of air intakes are visible above the C.205's engine cowling . The air intakes provide cooling for the engine, machine guns, exhaust stacks, and the oil radiator's circular elements. The two large bulges below the engine cowling housed the lower section of the engine's cylinder block. The inverted *V* configuration of the engine allowed Engineer Castoldi, through the introduction of bulged fairings, to obtain a very small frontal cross-section.

(Top Right) The Corbetta filter was composed of 12 semicircular fairings and an air intake valve that the pilot could hydraulically control. Normally, the filter remained closed when the aircraft was on the ground and flying at a low level so that sand in the air could be filtered by the circular, internal elements; thus, air arriving to the engine was free of material that could cause damage.

(Middle Right) The sand filter on the Veltro was identical to the one that Corbetta produced for the C.202 Folgore. Filter details and specifications were printed on a metal plate that was fixed on the front part of the filter. Introduced after the first version of the C.202 entered service, this installation proved to be efficient in a desert environment and became an integral feature for tropicalized aircraft that carried the *A.S.* suffix (Africa Settentrionale).

(Bottom Right) Part of the engine and its spark plugs are visible through the access panels and cooling inlets located above the exhausts. These panels allowed ground engineers to inspect the engine quickly without having to move the entire cowling.

(Below) Winter 1943—Sergente Maggiore Alverino Capatti poses on the nose of a 2ª Squadriglia Veltro of the ANR at Campoformido. Capatti was shot down by a P-38 Lightning on 28 March 1944. On 2 October 2004, Capatti's body and the remains of his Veltro were finally found near Ferrara and buried in his family's chapel.

The last access panel allowed for inspection of spark plugs and the engine bearer's right-hand side angled bar.

The motor oil return tube is visible through the spark plug inspection panel. The return tube carried the hot oil to the radiator to be cooled.

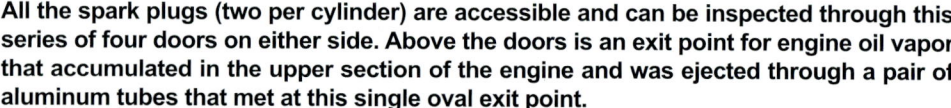

All the spark plugs (two per cylinder) are accessible and can be inspected through this series of four doors on either side. Above the doors is an exit point for engine oil vapor that accumulated in the upper section of the engine and was ejected through a pair of aluminum tubes that met at this single oval exit point.

# 3° Stormo's Badge

12

This complete view is of the starboard side engine cowling. A pair of small bulges above the engine cowling are rare to find on a Veltro; usually only the front one was visible. These bulges housed certain edges of the engine bearers, and the larger bulge on the nose was always present since it enclosed the edge of two water tubes. This Veltro was an ex-C.202 adapted to the new engine in the best possible manner, which justifies the presence of a horizontal panel line positioned halfway between the rear of the cowling and the vertical one perpendicular to it that is not found on the original production Veltros.

Three small circular hatches and three holes are centrally positioned above the cowling. The three small doors give access to (top to bottom) the engine oil filler cap, the undercarriage hydraulic oil filler cap, and the access tap for controlling motor oil dilution for cold engine start. The latter was only on III Series aircraft. The three holes are (from nose to tail) the insertion hole for the engine starter handle, the exit hole for the dynamo and fuel pump cooling air, and the exit hole for the 12.7 mm gun's outer casing. The upper intake seen on top of the cowling allowed air to flow into a bifurcated aluminum tube that went to cool the dynamo box and fuel pump and then exited from the central exit hole.

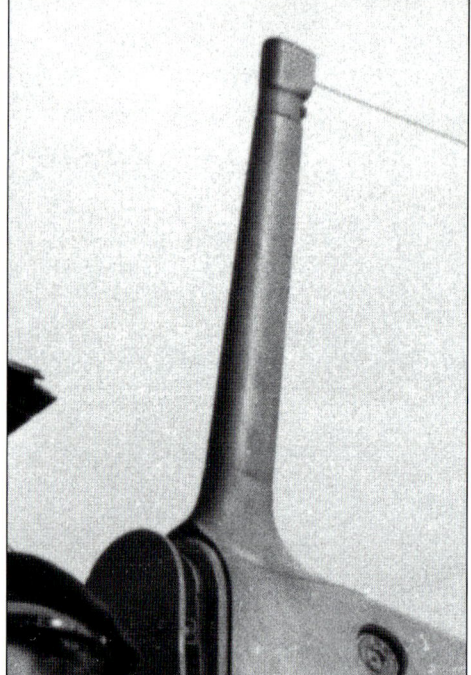

**(Top Left)** A new metal aerial mast (type Sares) was fitted to all III Series Veltros and varied in height. The antenna was hollow, and the aerial wire passed through the antenna and attached to the radio equipment in the rear fuselage. The Allocchio-Bacchini B.30 was an unreliable radio and forced pilots to signal by hand. (D'Amico e Valentini)

**(Top Right)** This aerial mast was typical on I Series C.205s and was already in use on the C.202 Folgore. The mast was made of wood and was sometimes given only a coat of transparent varnish.

**(Bottom Left)** For both the Royal Egyptian Air Force and Italian flying schools, a radical equipment change was necessary on post-war C.205s to bring communications in line with Americans. The SCR radio series introduced a hybrid antenna (RT.AN.104) and combined the attachment typical of Spitfires with a taller wartime style mast. In the case of this aircraft, an external cable parted from the top of the mast and entered the fuselage hump where it attached to the radio set.

A III Series Sares antenna mast is visible on a 3° Stormo's Veltro. The crew readies the plane for takeoff.

14

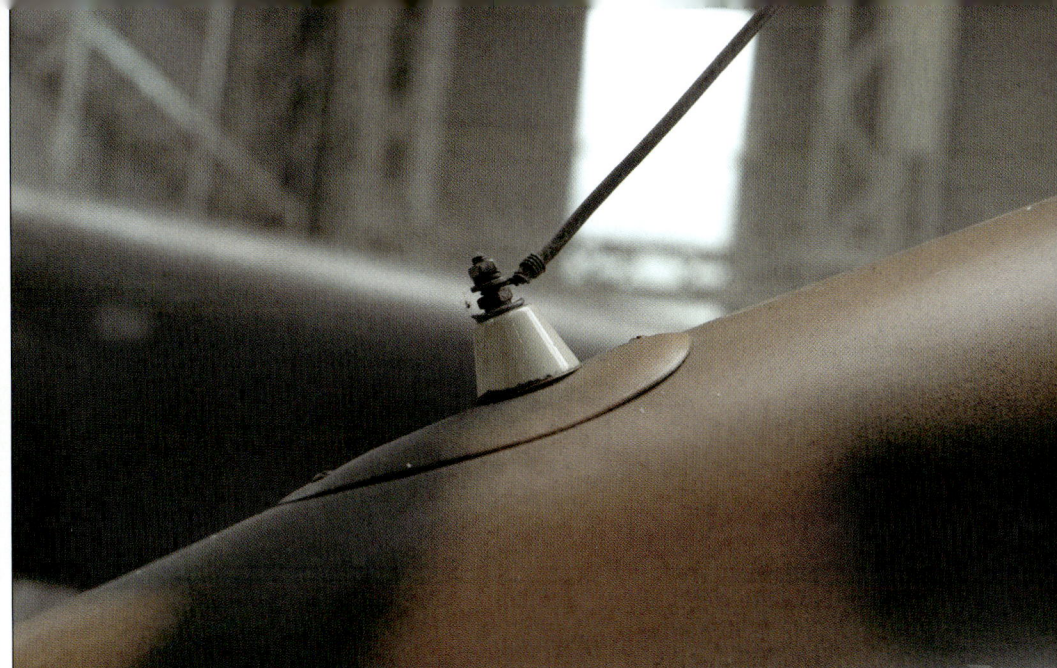

The metal cable antenna was strung taut between the mast and fin by a number of isolators that helped enhance reception and protect the unit from static electricity. Most isolators were made of porcelain, but some were made of glass. At times, the isolators were fitted with tension springs and protected by metallic cones.

This view shows the fin attaching point of the aerial antenna wire. The insulator consists of porcelain and metal.

The aerial cable entered the fuselage through a porcelain dipole that was covered with a black, rubber concertina gasket.

This Veltro MM.9357 displays its Veltro nickname on its fin. The plane will soon be delivered to its combat unit. The early style wood aerial mast with the fuselage dipole and the R.G. 42 direction finder loop antenna are located under the fuselage. (AleniaAermacchi)

The spinner was attached to a back plate and could be easily removed through an oval aperture found on the same plate that allowed maintenance or removal of the propeller hubs or blades.

Full details regarding the propeller blades were engraved at the blades' roots. Information listed includes serial number, version, manufacturer, and blade angle details.

Holes in the front spinner allowed cooling air to reach the propeller hub. The lightening holes of the spinner's internal structure and the rear disc are visible in this view.

A little over 1 cm of space separated the spinner from the engine cowling. This space was necessary for the rotating spinner to avoid interference from engine vibrations.

Piaggio's logo was carried on a limited number of Macchi C.205 propellers. The Piaggio P.2001 was taken directly from the P.1001 propeller that was used on the C.200 and C.202 and was designed by engineer Corradino D'Ascanio, the father of the helicopter in Italy as well as the Vespa Scooter.

Macchi designed a special logo for the blades, and the logo decal was applied at the center of the blades' front face.

This front view shows the design finesse of the P.2001 propeller blade and its twist from its root to its extreme point.

17

(Above) Spent cartridges and links could be removed through a pair of round doors in the fuselage that provided direct access to the collector boxes. Armorers had to recover these brass cartridges because they were considered strategic recyclable materials. As this material became more scarce, the cartridges were made from lacquered iron.

(Left) This close-up shows the installation of the Breda-Società Anonima Fabbrica Armi Torino (SAFAT) 12.7 mm guns above the Veltro's nose. These guns were stepped to facilitate the installation of ammunition boxes and spent cartridge collectors. A total of 400 rounds could be carried for each gun. Also visible are the synchronization mechanism, the re-cocking rods, and the pneumatic piping. The guns' barrels ran through different lengths of cooling tubes. These varied lengths compensated for the guns' stepped positions and allowed both exit points to be in line above the engine cowling. The SAFAT's barrels did not extend beyond the cowling outlets, however.

(Below) The two SAFAT blast tubes were often painted in a heat-resistant black paint.

This C.205 nose is without its cowling. The two 12.7 mm machine guns were fitted just above the main fuel tank, and the tank's refuelling tap is located just beside the left machine gun. The black rods that reach the rear part of the upper engine are the synchronization devices.

The SAFAT machine guns (later built by Breda) were easy to maintain and had good precision and range. The 12.7 mm gun essentially was an enlarged version of the 7.7 mm gun except the smaller version was less efficient. An efficient belt feed helped make the 12.7 mm gun more accurate and reliable, and the belts were filled according to an individual pilot's demands. Ordinary cartridges could be interspersed by a number of armor piercing, tracer, incendiary, and explosive bullets. Firing through the propeller arc limited the guns' rate of fire, however. Optimum firing range was 500 meters for the 7.7 mm gun and 700 meters for the 12.7 mm gun. (A.M. Museum, Vigna di Valle)

This original explosive type 12.7 mm x 81SR cartridge was produced at the Lazio Bombrini-Parodi Delfino factory in 1943. Its metal shell is painted olive green. This particular cartridge came from a C.205, MM.92205, flown by Serg. Magg. Garavaldi of the 1° Gruppo ANR. Garavaldi was shot down on 14 May 1944, and was recovered with the remains of his fighter on 5 August 2000, at Molinella. (Bologna)

With the central cowling removed, the 12-liter liquid refrigerant tank is visible and painted green. Ahead of the tank is the cooling air tube for the dynamo and fuel pump. Below the tank and tube is the 36-liter oil tank, painted brown. The R.A. Intava Rotring mineral oil was filled through the right-hand side.

The oval hole, located on the left side of the plane, was an air outlet for the fuel filter and the port machine gun.

The compressor fairing, painted blue-black, and engine mounts were easily accessible with the cowling removed. The two semi-circular supports, painted silver, were electrical cable attachments. Fixed to the angled V-shaped support, the water pressure valve, painted brown, and the static tension regulator, painted black, are visible.

This visual aiming sight was positioned above the plane's nose and provided the pilot with a secondary aid in case the reflection gun sight broke down.

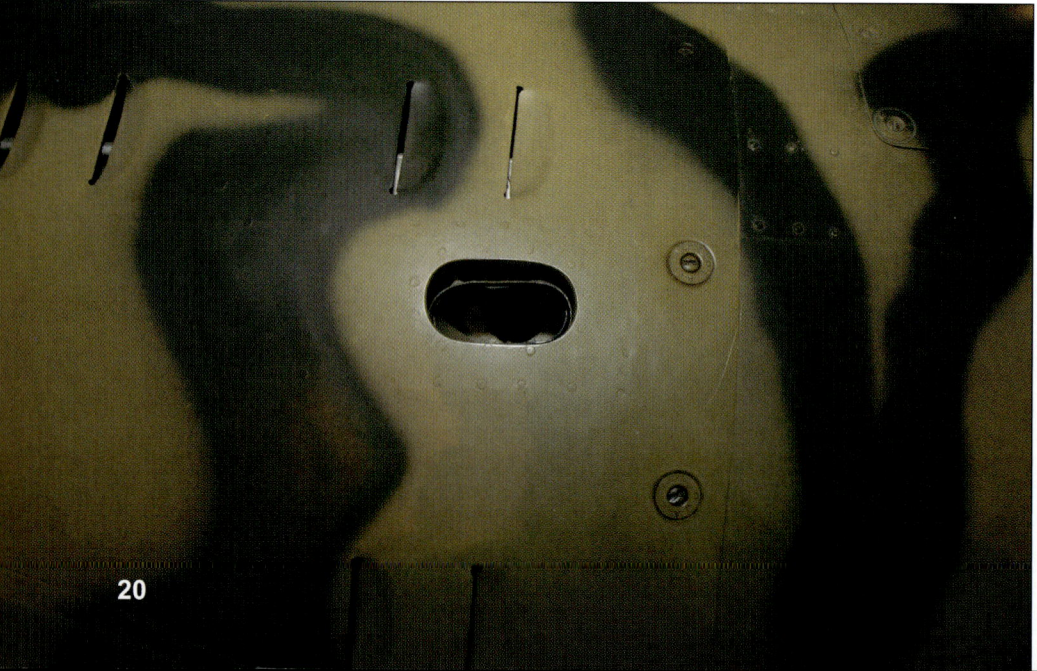

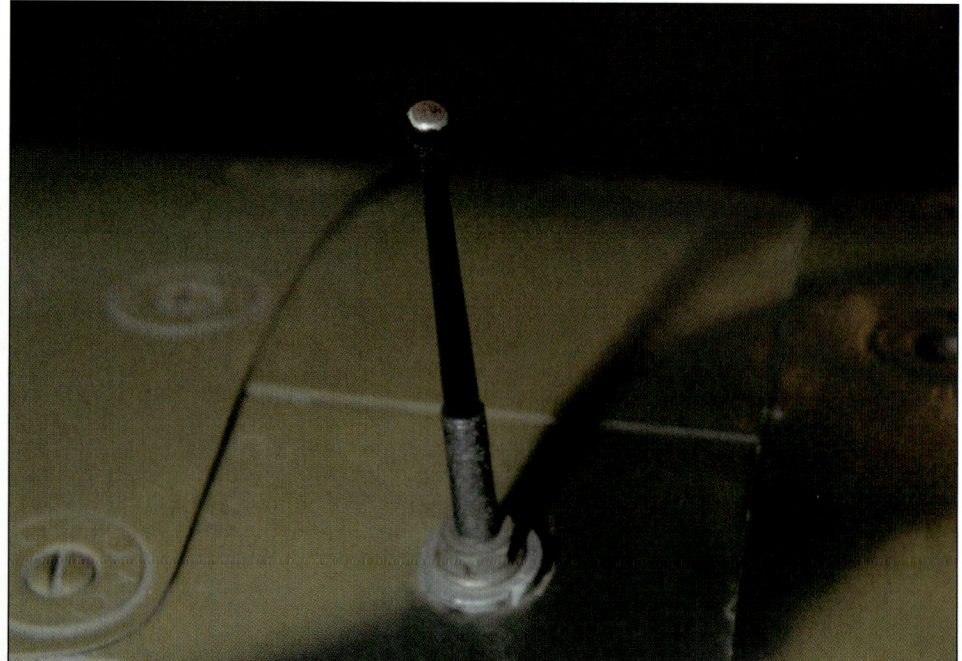

The cowling is completely dismantled from the plane, and all its inspection panels and the central air intake are visible. The cowling is internally painted with a matte green primer that is not the original paint. The original anti-corrosion green was a lighter, nearly grey tone.

A folding stick was fitted ahead of the spinner and calibrated the magnetic compass on a scalable platform.

A small, semi-circular air intake, located between the gun outlets, provided cooling air to the Zenit Type II dynamic compressor, responsible for running the pneumatic aircraft systems. The cooling fins and compressor head are visible inside the air intake.

These different views are of the standard fastener used in various points of the C.205's nose for locking the upper and lower engine cowlings. Although they were strong and rigid, the fasteners were easy to open and unlock.

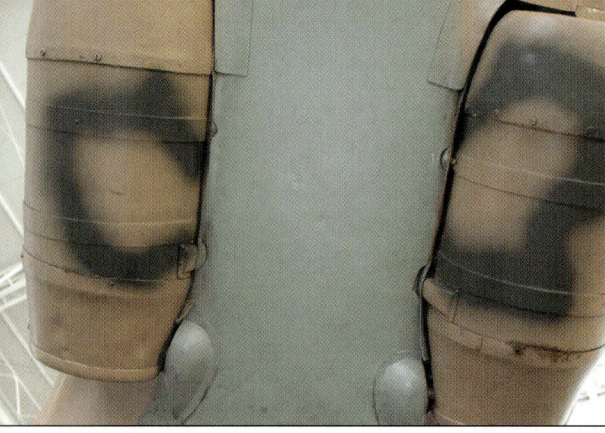

A pair of barrel-type oil radiators are positioned below the nose of the plane. The two bulges that house the rear flap's opening and closing mechanism are to the rear of the radiators. The radiators were separated from the rest of the lower cowling to minimize movements caused by engine vibration. In fact, the radiators were directly fixed by an elastic metal structure to the lower part of the engine.

The radiator element was a honeycomb construction, was semi-buried to reduce aerodynamic drag, and was separated to enable a higher dynamic air intake into the radiator and its refrigerant liquid.

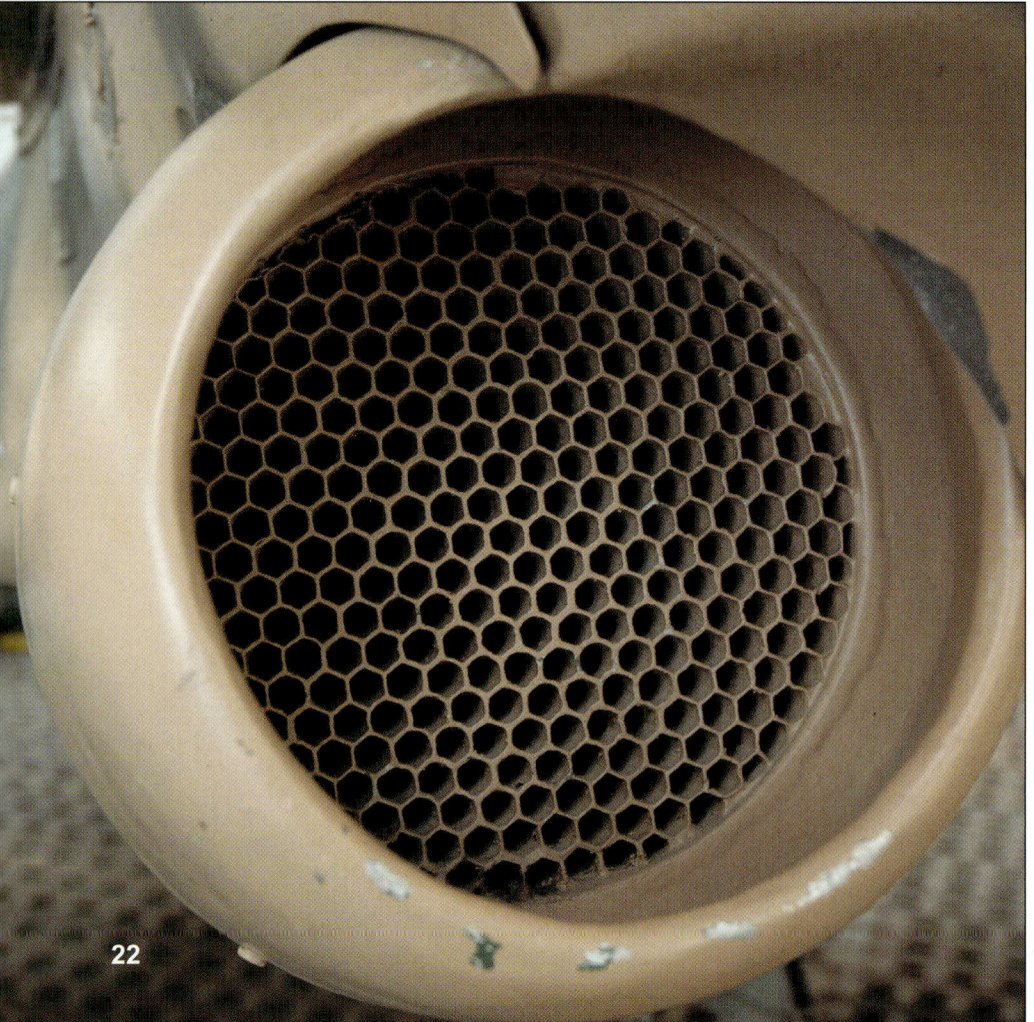

The pair of apertures below the spinner cooled the lower part of the engine, where the tube that carried air coming from the compressor was positioned.

A damaged DB.605 A engine from a C.205 has been disembarked with its bearers at the Lonate Pozzolo facility. (AleniaAermacchi)

Early Macchi C.205s had the engine oil vent placed on the right. The vent was formed from a single cylindrical tube similar to what was on the C.202. The C.205's outlet was positioned further aft, however.

The intermediate oil vent is formed from two tubes that joined at the height of the spark plug access panels and combined into a wide and thin air exhaust.

This exhaust outlet is the one that is typically found on the C.205 III and VI Series. Two tubes form the outlet, and they merge into one larger, oval exhaust. (D'Amico and Valentini)

Various air outlets are visible on the starboard side of this C.205, MM.92289, that just landed at Dübendorf, Switzerland, and has seen better days. (Flieger Flab Museum-Dübendorf)

Intermediate Oil Vent

The side cowling had an access panel for inspecting the oil radiator's bearers.

The engine oil outlet clearly shows the two tubes from which the outlet is composed.

A separation exists between the oil barrel radiator and the cowling to avoid contact between parts caused by engine vibrations.

Oil radiators had a hydraulically controlled partitioning flap at the rear. III and VI Series Veltros had this feature. The pilot could not choose to increase or decrease oil-cooling air on I Series.

(Top photographs) The C.205's main undercarriage was similar to the undercarriage on the C.202, which presented minimal internal and externals differences. The compressed air tubes commanded the brakes, which divided in two, at a point close to the leg's fork. Usually, the legs were finished in a glossy medium grey except for an aluminum rim. The red object in the top left photo is a security block for the undercarriage that was installed by museum personnel.

Located below the starboard exhaust stacks is an external power socket for the aircraft. The polarities are clearly marked. This socket was usually only used on the field when a small generator was available. An inertia hand starting system, which was turned by ground crew personnel, was more commonly used.

While these Dunlop Aero Standard tires fitted to the C.205 at Venegono are the right size, they are historically incorrect. Pirelli tires were used during the war.

Fabbrica Articoli Scientifici e Tecnici (FAST) made the C.205's wheels, and they were fitted with Pirelli-made tires. This C.205 was damaged during a hard landing at Dübendorf. Its hydraulic ram was bent on impact, but the plane's wheel and tire details are visible.

Pirelli *Aeroplano* type tires for the C.205 measured 600x200x216. Two tire types were available: one smooth, one with vertical grooves.

The attachment and fixture of the retraction folders for the wheel doors were complex, especially the small upper attachments.

The anti-torsion compass of the main left leg and the collar fixed on the pin absorbed considerable landing force, especially since the wheels were filled to half or medium pressure, and the undercarriage had a wide track.

The C.205's main wheel doors were slightly different from the doors on the Folgore. Two grooves were added to the upper part of the door, and the lower part of the door had a bulge that housed the wheel hub and brake piping.

Without armament, munitions, fuel, oil, and ordnance, the Veltro at Venegono is lighter than a battle-ready aircraft, as the extended shock absorber shows.

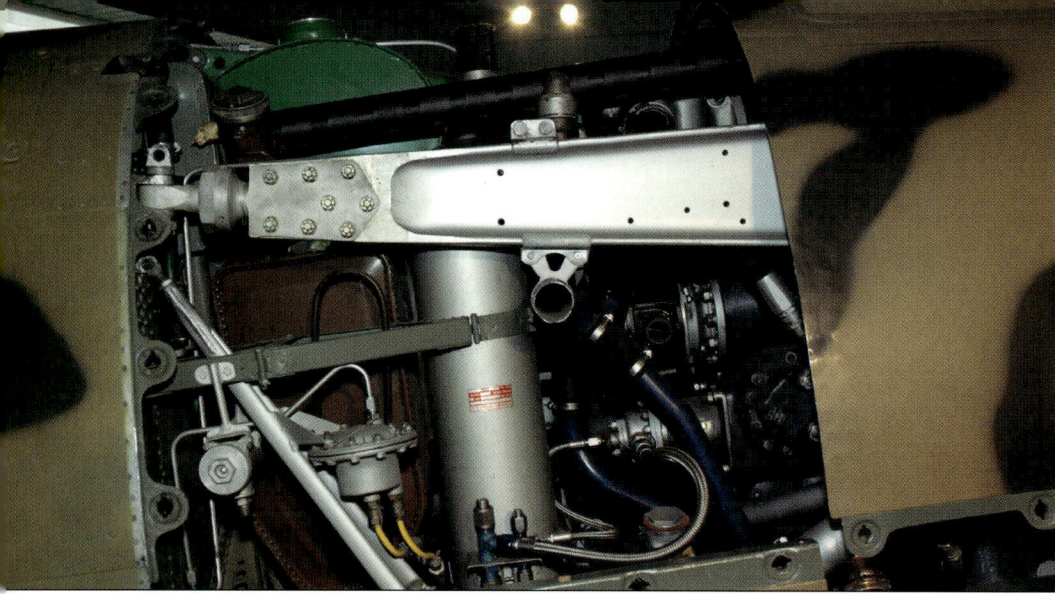

The fuselage without the central cowling shows the forged Duraluminum engine mounts that are fixed directly to the robust steel firewall. The engine consists of an original German DB-605 A, serial number 298342. Immediately to the right of the oil tank is a metal-colored cylinder with two yellow tubes coming out of it. This cylinder is the E.C. fuel injector that starts the pneumatic system.

Apart from the green refrigerant and brown motor oil tanks, the large oil tank for the undercarriage retraction system is visible. The blue tube with an open rubber handle is the stopper for the air intake, positioned above the engine cowling. In between the replica machine guns are the magnets and distribution group where the engine's original identification tag is attached.

The Daimler Benz engine was composed of two banks of six cylinders in an inverted V-form banked at 60°. The engine could provide 1,475 hp and weighed 780 kg.

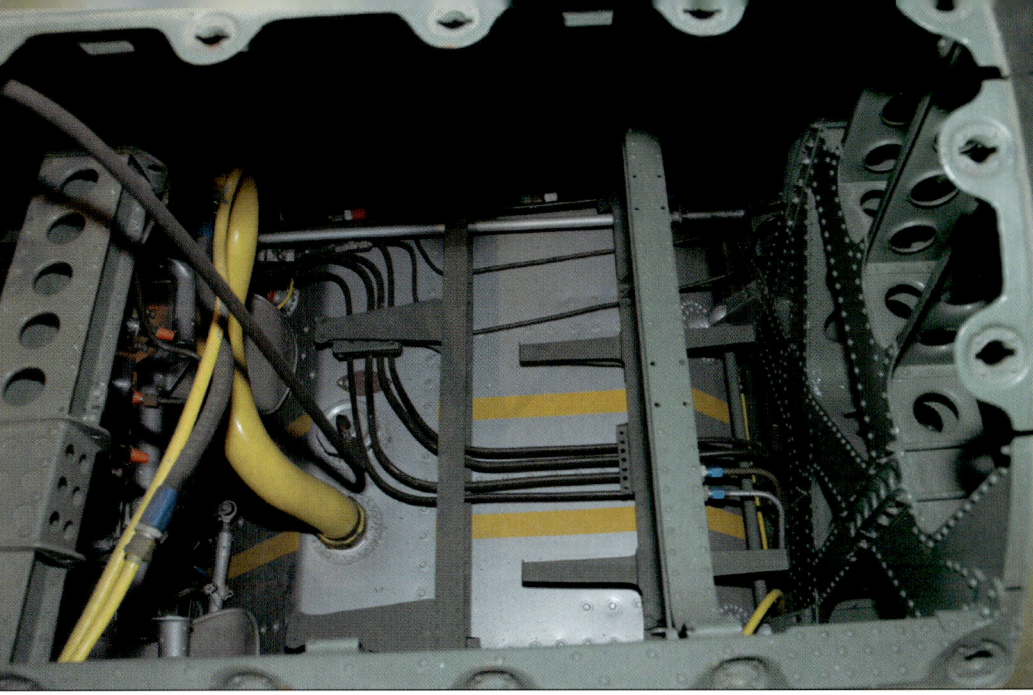

With the armament missing, the principal fuel tank is easily accessible.

Also easily eaccessible is the fuel tank's filler pipe. Some of the instruments rear sides are visible, but not all the instruments are original.

By removing various windscreen area panels, the crew could easily maintain the onboard guns that were fixed to internal crossbars. No such armament installations are found on the Veltro at Venegono.

The two inspection panels on the starboard side of the central cowling allowed ground personnel to top up these tanks with special cans without having to remove the whole cowling.

This tap was used for starting up the engine at low temperatures, which was accomplished by thinning engine oil through the flow of fuel into the oil system. The bottom left picture shows the tap. The bottom center picture shows the access panel for the tap in the closed position.

Despite all the outlets on its nose, the Veltro had a clean, aerodynamic shape. This appearance was applied to the tear-shaped levers and access panels on the wings and fuselage.

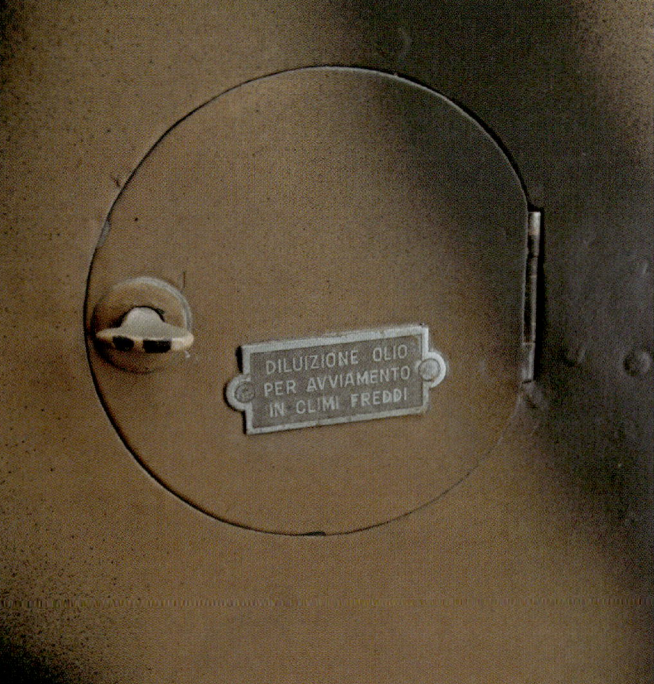

A small panel above the central cowling provided easy access to the filler cap of the refrigerant. Cooling system components were always colored green, and the cap could be opened using a hexagonal key or the other end of the engine starter handle.

The filler cap to the compressed air system could be found at the end of the starboard fuselage-to-wing joint. The air system was charged on the ground from an external cylinder and supplied armament and brake systems.

The pilot could use the 8-shaped exit holes in the fuselage skin, on the starboard side and in line with the wings, for signalling by firing his twin-barreled Very pistol. Six different colored cartridges were fitted on the right-hand side of the pilot's seat inside the cockpit.

A water pressure valve used the air exit, which was protected by a small fairing close to the engine oil filler cap.

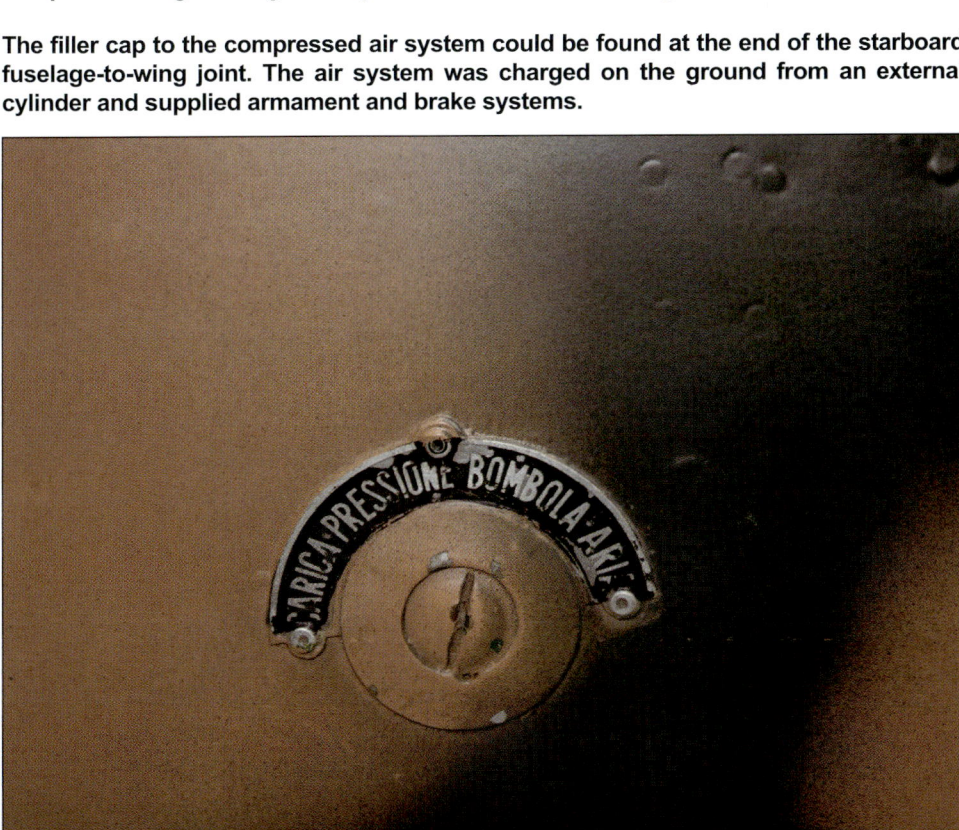

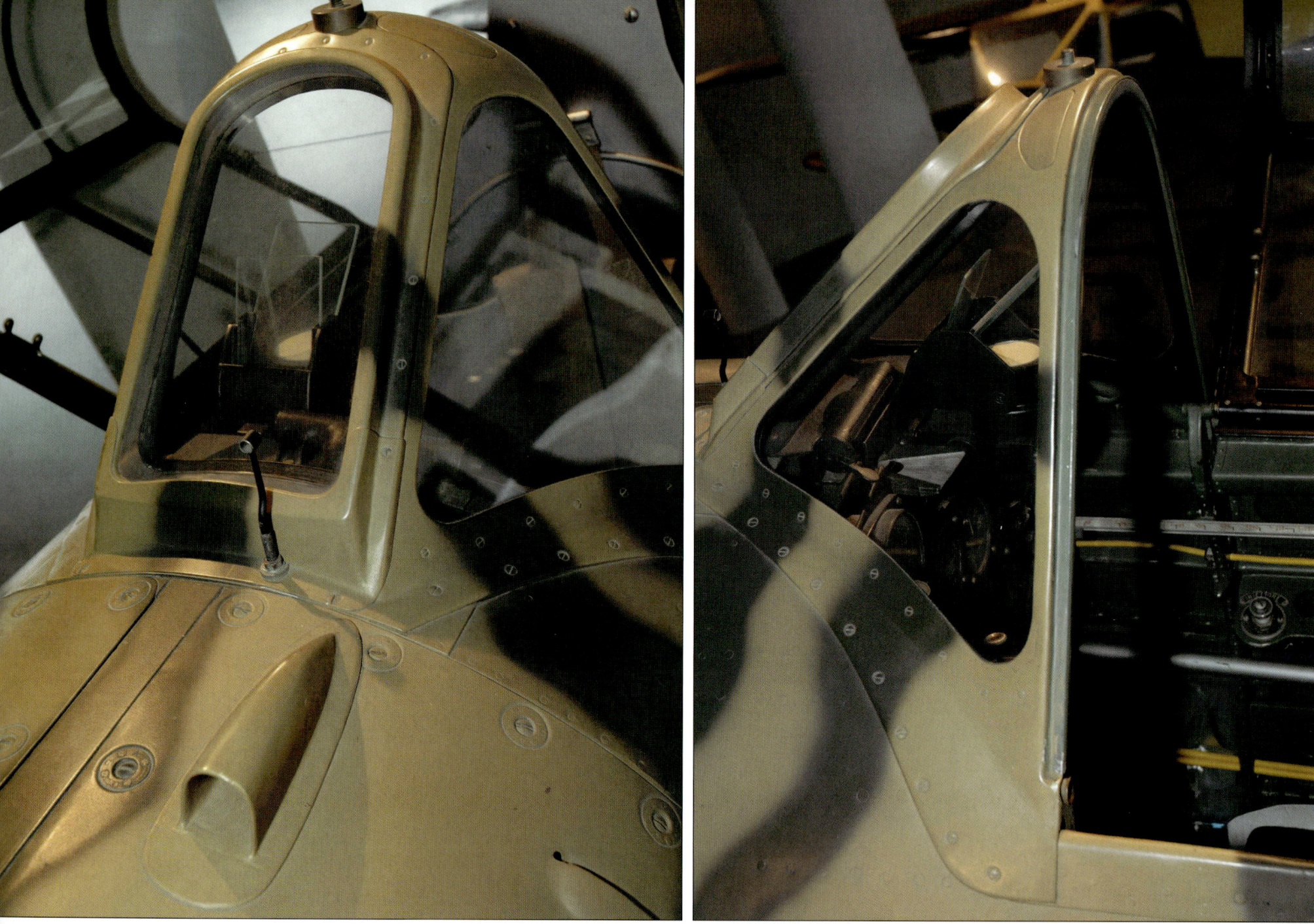

The C.205's windscreen was fitted with an armored glass plate type Vis 1 mounted inside the front panel. The side panels were not armored. The large air intake on the port side of the windscreen provided fresh air into the cockpit and could be regulated through a cylindrical aperture mounted to the left of the gunsight

A pair of spring hand-holds were cut out at the top of the windscreen frame and helped the pilot enter and leave the cockpit.

A support for the rear view mirror (mirror missing in this example) was fitted between the spring hand-holds.

The cockpit canopy swung 90° toward starboard and was held in place by a steel cable to one of the armored headrest supports.

The canopy, in closed position, reveals the cut-out corners for the closing/opening inside hinges and the lateral shape of the armoured front windscreen.

Protrusions

The two protrusions visible in the glazing in the foreground served as handles to slide the panel backward.

These two views are of the Venturi tube, named after Italian scientist Giovanni Battista Venturi, that is fitted to the C.205 Veltro on the starboard side below the windscreen. The contemporary view to the right shows the tube through which pressurized air enters to power the bank indicator and horizontal gyroscope. (Flieger Flab Museum—Dübendorf).

By removing the copious radio compartment inspection door immediately aft of the hump, the crew could access the radio and electrical equipment. A pair of Tudor batteries was placed close to the survoltor, the large metallic cylinder visible below the elevator control rod. This element served to heavily increase the tension within the system to ensure perfect functioning of the large radio B.30 valves. (AleniaAermacchi)

A wartime Veltro has its radio and first aid access panels open. The first aid access panel is inverted 180° in respect to the panel on the C.202 and as seen on the three surviving C.205s. From left to right, the three units mounted on a bracket are the radio receiver, the radio direction finder Type R.G.42, and the radio transmitter. (AleniaAermacchi)

The Macchi C.205, MM.92214, which was the protagonist of the famous flight over Rome on 6 October 1942, gets an extensive overhaul inside a hangar at Lecce Galatina during the Co-Belligerent period. The first aid access panel on this plane is turned toward the radio access panel. (A.M.)

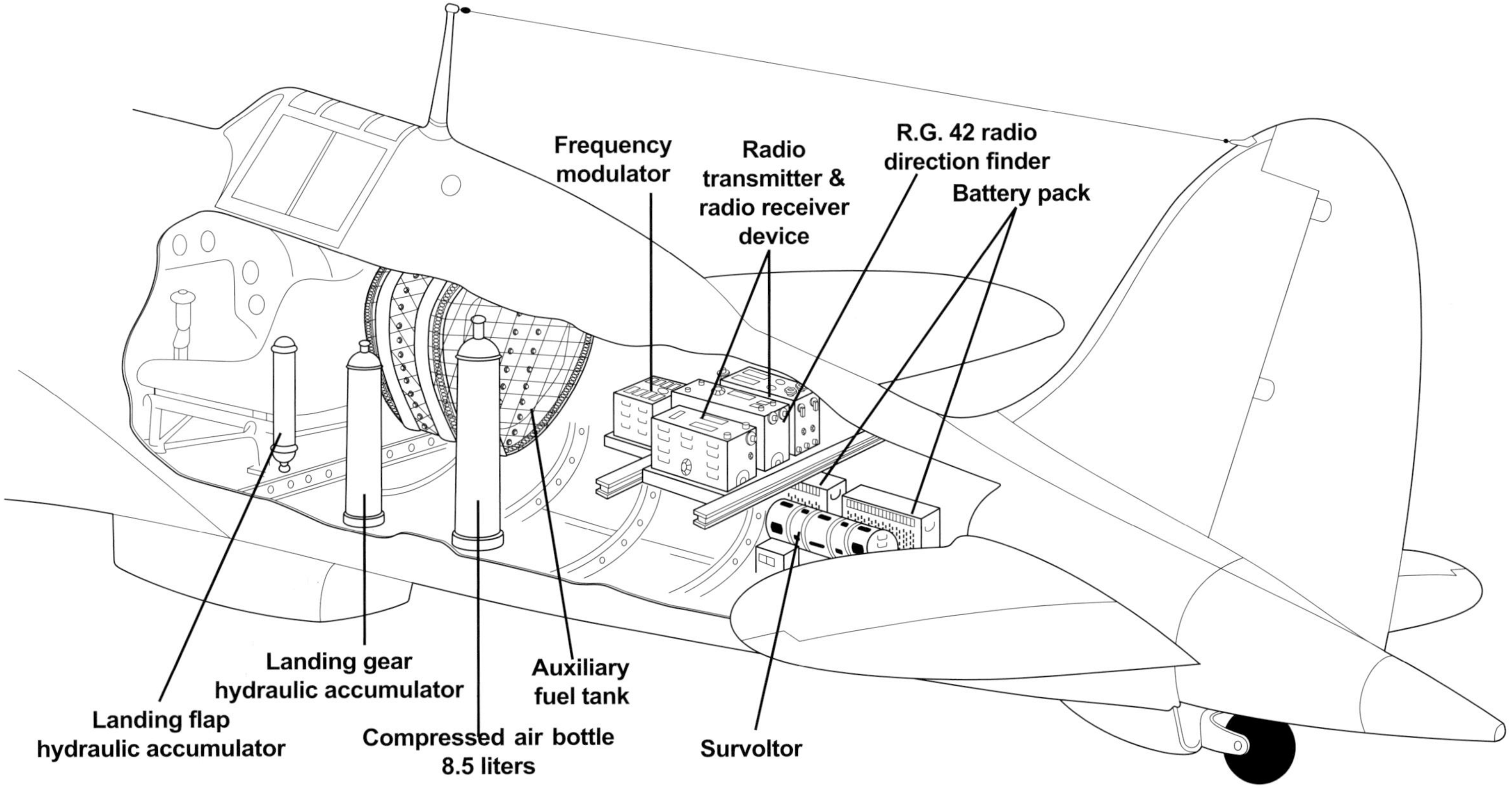

Frequency modulator

Radio transmitter & radio receiver device

R.G. 42 radio direction finder

Battery pack

Landing flap hydraulic accumulator

Landing gear hydraulic accumulator

Compressed air bottle 8.5 liters

Auxiliary fuel tank

Survoltor

This recreated view shows the inner installations of the C.205's fuselage. Located in the rear part of the tail boom are the radio devices and electrical installations that were easily mainteined by accessing two trapezoidal access panels.

(Top) The complicated C.205 undercarriage bay formed part of the lower engine mount, and a myriad of cables and connection pipes passed through it. This construction allowed for quick and easy inspection, but it also continuously accumulated a good amount of dust and dirt in a delicate area. Because of this problem, final C.202 and C.205 versions were provided with a pair of fairings in thin metal sheeting that enclosed this bay. These fairings were molded to allow the undercarriage mechanism to function and were also provided with two inspection panels.

(Bottom Right) The mechanism that retracted into the two central doors to enclose the undercarriage bay was highly simple. As the main wheel retracted, it pushed the tab on the three cylinders to close the door.

The two handles inside the middle of the undercarriage bay were manually activated on the ground prior to engine start. The handle (right-hand undercarriage bay) raised the brushes of the smaller starter motor to neutralize it. The other handle set off the injector. This handle formed part of the inertia starting procedure and coupled the started motor with the engine. Once the engine was turned, the left handle was released to lower the starter motor brushes into place. Together with the two handles, the pilot activated two more located on the lower instrument panel to provide a quick cleaning of the fuel filters and to facilitate the engine starting at temperatures below 15° C, which resulted in a quicker engine start-up.

This view shows the left undercarriage bay. In the top right corner is the blue tube for cooling the fuel filters, and the silver tube is for the compressor air inlet.

# House of Savoy Coat of Arms

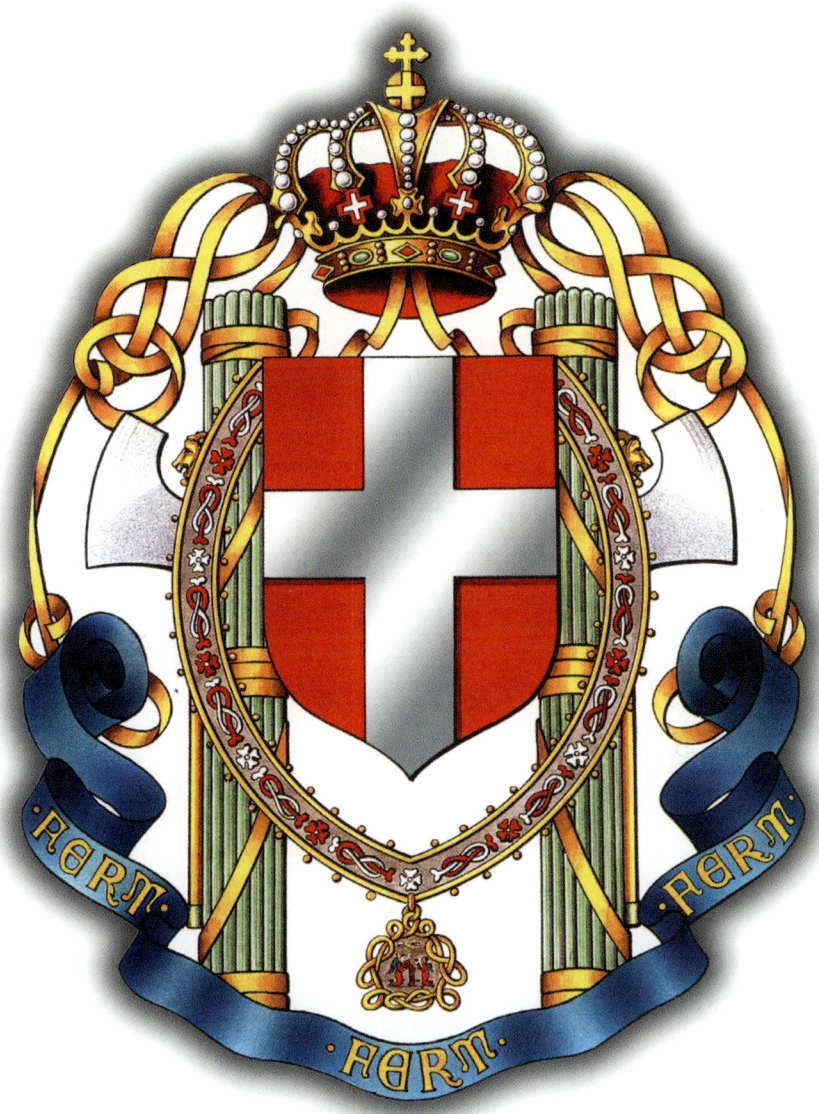

The House of Savoy Coat of Arms was the symbol of the Italian monarchy until 1946. The symbol was placed between the arms of the white cross painted on the rudder of the C.205.

The undercarriage bay's left side houses a ubiquitous piping system. The pincer attached to the engine mount forms part of the undercarriage mechanism and is hooked up with the appropriate support, found on the main wheel leg.

The octagon cap between the two undercarriage bays allowed quick oil release from the tank and barrel-shaped radiators, which were doubled to lubricate six cylinders each.

The large fairing ahead of the radiator houses a hydraulic piston that lowers the landing flaps. Further forward are two small panels that provide fuel filter access. The offset closes the tap for quick release of fuel from the main tank.

The 40-liter fuel tank's quick release tap is visible in this photo. Also visible are three vent tubes that serve as fuel and water drains.

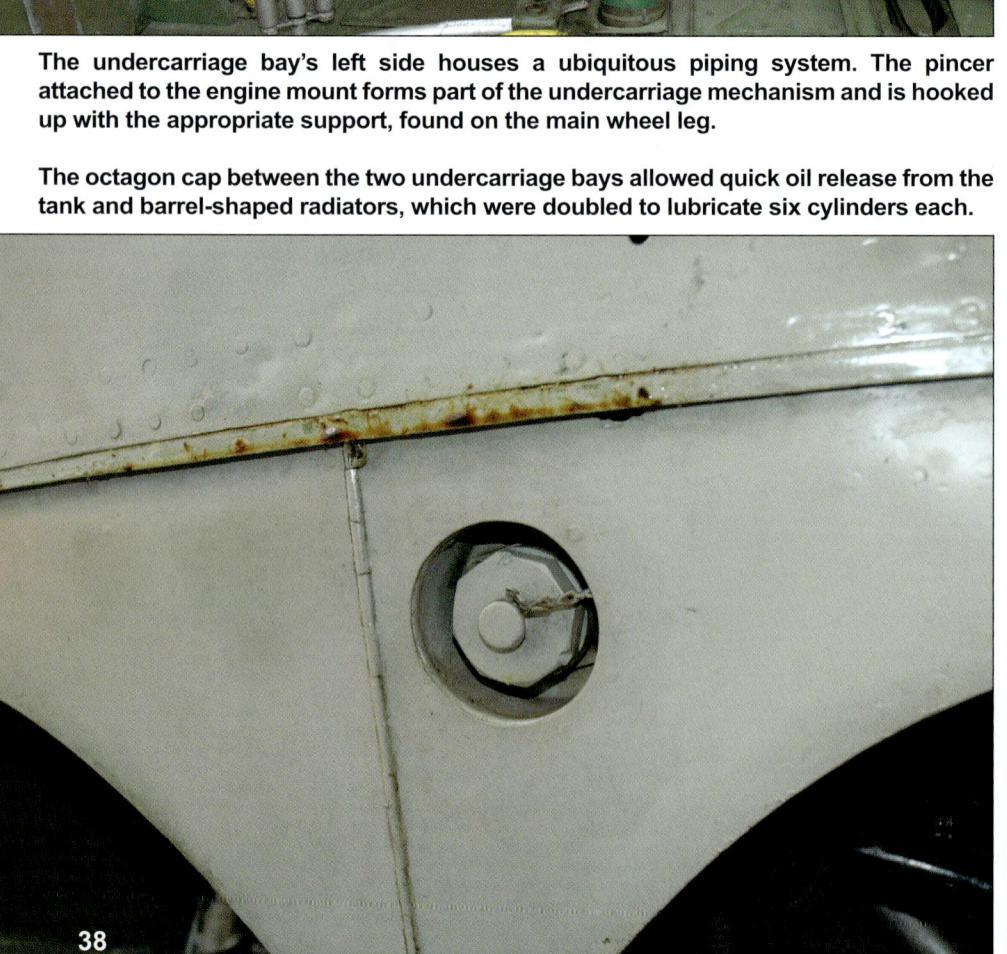

The retraction piston leg of the main undercarriage is painted brown, like all components of the hydraulic system. In the side of the perforated structure is a spring that maintained tension on the two central undercarriage bay doors.

## 5° Stormo's Badge

The large green tube was the flow tube for refrigeration liquid to the engine radiator. Separate from this tube was an identical tube inside the opposite undercarriage bay where water flowed back to the radiator. In the foreground is the hole that was used to insert a jack to lift the aircraft during maintenance or gun calibration. The tail was lifted to bring the aircraft into a horizontal position by inserting a tube through the lifting holes, positioned immediately ahead of the tailplane.

"Veltro„
serie = III
P.V. Kg. 2587

A number of I Series C.205s and all III Series C.205s carried this Veltro logo. The logo was stenciled on and retouched by hand. Indications of the aircraft's empty weight (Peso a Vuoto—P.V.) varied from one aircraft to another by a few kilograms.

Reconditioned aircraft during the Co-Belligerent period often were extensively repainted. Thus, style and character dimension varied considerably.

M.M.92166
AS

The serial number painted on the Venegono C.205 has correct dimensions but incorrect character style. The periods in the A.S. suffix are missing, and the *A* should be rounder.

Early I Series C.205 aircraft carried the typical Macchi inscription on the fin that was found on the C.202. The V initially stood for Veloce (fast) to indicate a modified C.202, not an entirely new aircraft.

MM. 9546

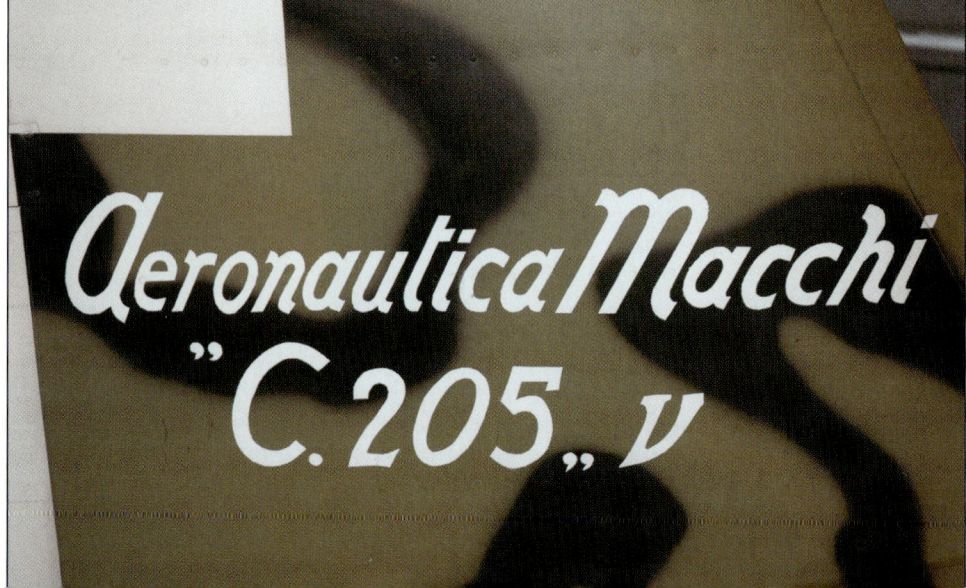

AeronauticaMacchi
"C.205„ v

(Top) When all C.205s transferred to flying schools and Veltros introduced the all-silver finish, markings returned to an old style, adapted to new conditions, through the use of the old C.202 stencils. Wording, including service load (Carico Utile—C.U.) on the tail and serial number below the lifting hole, was the classic Azzurro 11 (blue) that was in use during WWII.

(Bottom Left) The fin and rudder of the C.202 in Co-Belligerent markings at Vigna di Valle include the rampant horse (Cavallino Rampante) and the numerals for the 9° Gruppo of the 4° Stormo.

(Bottom Center) The Venegono example carries the Veltro logo at port and the full wording at starboard. Also visible is the Savoy Coat or Arms directly in the middle of the Savoy Cross.

(Bottom Right) This detail shows the swallow-tail shape of the corrugated reinforcement that strengthened the tail end of the fuselage.

41

Pratica di Mare, 2001—This C.205's serial number is incomplete. Two small, red arrows appear in this photo. These arrows were used for aligning the fixed horizontal tail surfaces that could be trimmed in flight by the pilot in order to lighten aerodynamic load on the longitudinal controls. The strobe light fitted to the tail cone was white.

This I Series C.205, MM.9314, has white data on its fin at wartime. (AleniaAermacchi)

The C.205 Type D tail wheel was introduced on the C.202 midway through its production run. A molded, light metal plate sealed off the bay. The Spiga tire measured 300 x 100 cm.

The tail wheel structure was usually left as natural metal or painted aluminum, but some tail wheel structures were painted anti-corrosion green, as discovered during excavations of shot down C.205s.

This view shows the torsion tube of the tailplane, connected to the other elevator.

Aerodynamic compensators were different from their predecessors as they had three metal clasps of different sizes at the bottom and removed the previous three metal rectangular clasp coverings of the elevator. Three square-hinge inspection panels are now fitted here.

Aerodynamic compensators at the end of tail surfaces were introduced on the C.202 to compensate flutter problems, which sometimes led to the loss of these surfaces in flight.

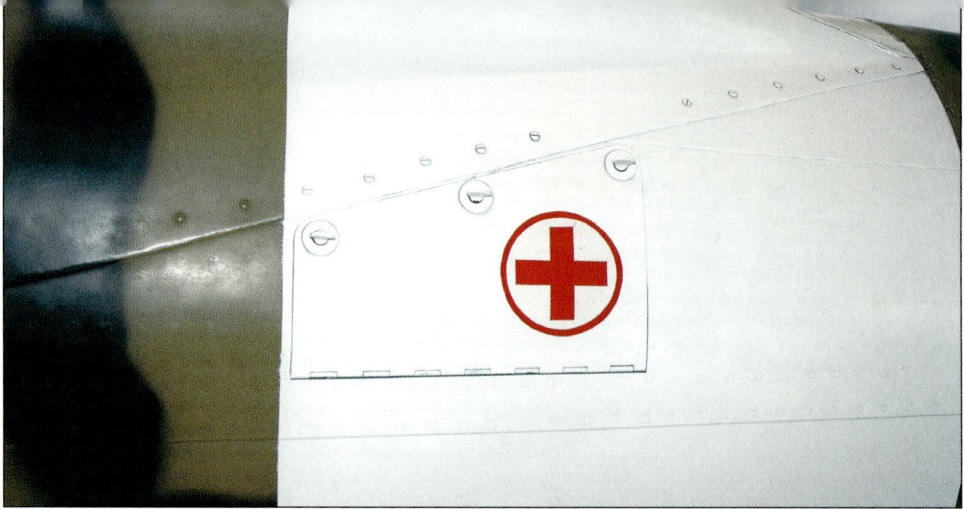

The First Aid Access panel on the Vigna di Valle C.205 is horizontally flipped in respect to the standard Veltros. This area was originally the C.202 fuselage. The panel is opened by three turn screws, and a similar panel on the other side of the fuselage is secured by three sprung screws. The red cross that indicated the First Aid compartment was usually without the red circle, as seen in this photo, or even painted on a plain Verde Oliva Scuro 2 background.

The Vigna di Valle C.205 has its original equipment in the state it was at the time it was slated for transfer to Egypt. The plane has the American T.R. 5043 radio receiver/transmitter fitted on the typical C.202 internal bracket. To the right of the set is a blue, 8.5-liter cylinder that supplies the FAST pneumatic system that was recharged while the aircraft was on the ground. During its normal function, this cylinder continuously pressurized through a small Zenit Type II° compressor, supplying both braking and armament systems.

This badge represented the Fourth Stormo during the Liberation War.

The front flap has a fixed, predetermined incidence and is fitted with a pair of strengthening rods.

The water-cooling radiator has a pair of hydraulic pistons to control the rear flap.

The radiator carries a horizontal corrugation and a support for fitting the front and rear fairings.

This plate, fixed to the radiator's central element, shows the radiator's long operational life. Made in March 1944, it was overhauled by manufacturer Seconda Mona for its exportation to Egypt in February 1948.

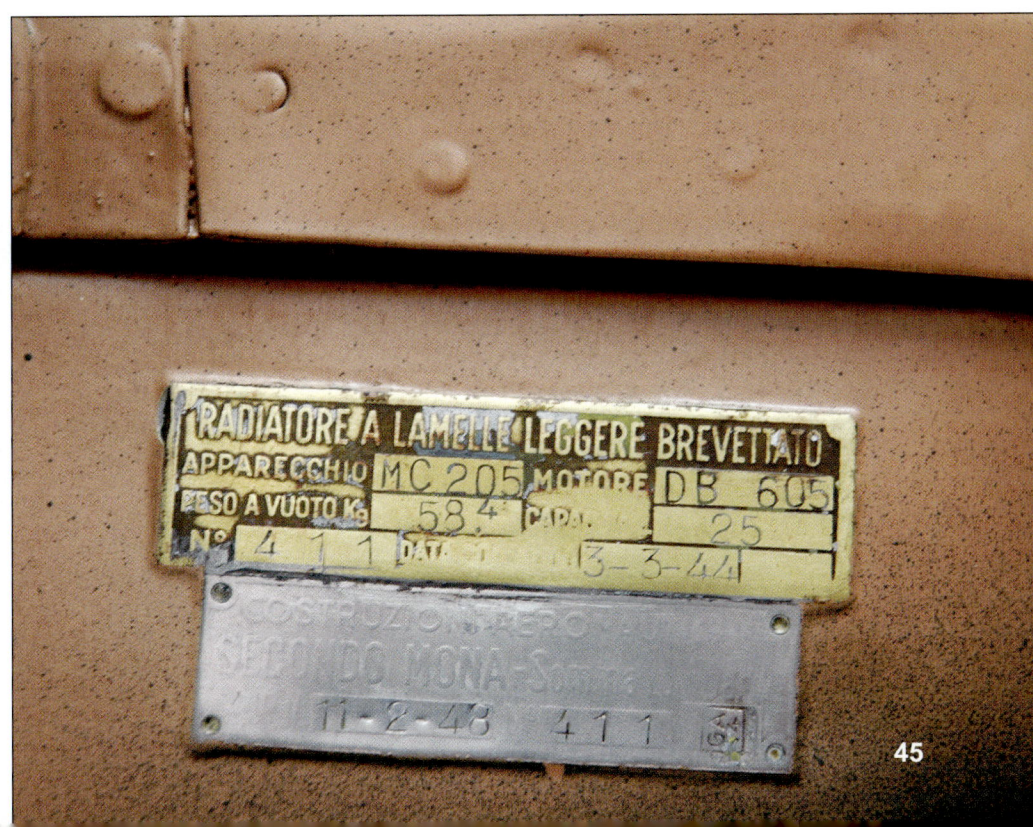

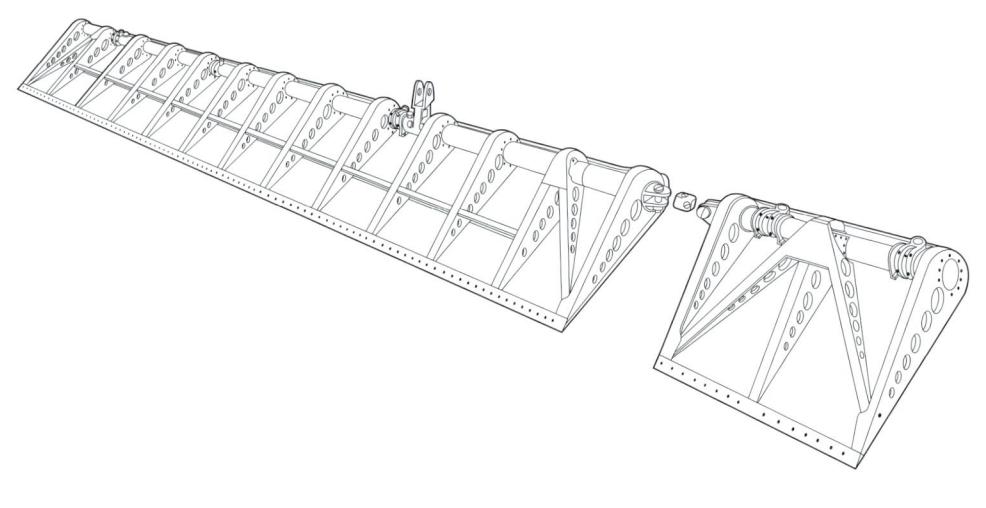

The Macchi's landing flaps were composed of one longer portion separated from a smaller one. The flaps were made of aluminum. Once in the parking area and with the engine off, the flaps remained in the up position due to a hydraulic pressure accumulator.

Maggiore Ruspoli (center of photo) and two RAF officers at Gino Lisa airfield in Foggia go over his leaflet supply, inserted in-between C.205's, MM.92214, flaps. Camouflage paint covers the white fuselage band, and a tricolor roundel is painted on the plane. (Luigi Iacomino).

This view shows details of the unit and a close-up of the end of the C.205 flap, composed of two parts that moved together. The smaller, rectangular flap is not curved at its trailing edge, as it is often incorrectly represented.

The C.205's flap was hydraulically actuated to a maximum 45° downward angle that could be lowered in 5° increments. Thanks to a pressure accumulator inserted in the system, the flap retracted automatically if speed exceeded 200 km/h. The opposite happened if the speed fell below this mark.

(Top Left) Veltro fuel tanks consisted of four units with a 430-liter total capacity. The main 270-liter tank was situated below the fuselage-mounted machine guns. Two 40-liter tanks were fitted inside the wing roots. These tanks were filled through a single inlet situated ahead of the windscreen with the smaller tanks linked to the main tank by pipes that passed through the undercarriage bay. A supplementary tank was situated behind the pilot's seat and could hold 80 liters. This tank was filled through an opening below the aerial mast and on the port side of the cockpit fairing.

(Top Right) Summer 1943—Ground crew from the 95ª Squadriglia (3° Stormo) refuel one of the few C.205 III Series the unit had received at Cerveteri. Access panels to the fuel tanks are open. The technician working on the nose area carefully checks the level of refrigerant through the rear end of the starting handle that was specially fitted with a hexagonal key. The refrigerant consisted of 50 percent demineralized water, 45 percent glycol, and 5 percent anti-corrosion agent.

(Bottom Right) Fuel used on the C.205 was Type B.4 of 87 to 100 octane. This value referred to the quantity of anti-detonation lead found in the fuel and was marked within red and white triangles that indicated the refueling point with the initials B 92. During the flight tests at Venegono and at Lonate Pozzolo, Macchi generally used 100-octane fuel.

47

The two 40-liter tanks were situated inside the wing roots, on the side of the other 270-liter tank. The tanks were fitted into position through rectangular panels below the wings , although they could be easily inspected from above through a circular panel (shown in top right photo) situated halfway along the wing to the fuselage joint.

The four tanks of the Macchi C.205 were made from aluminum, and the SEMAPE firm made the self-sealing interior treatment. Just two refuelling points are visible—one for the rear tank and one for the other three tanks, which were interconnected.

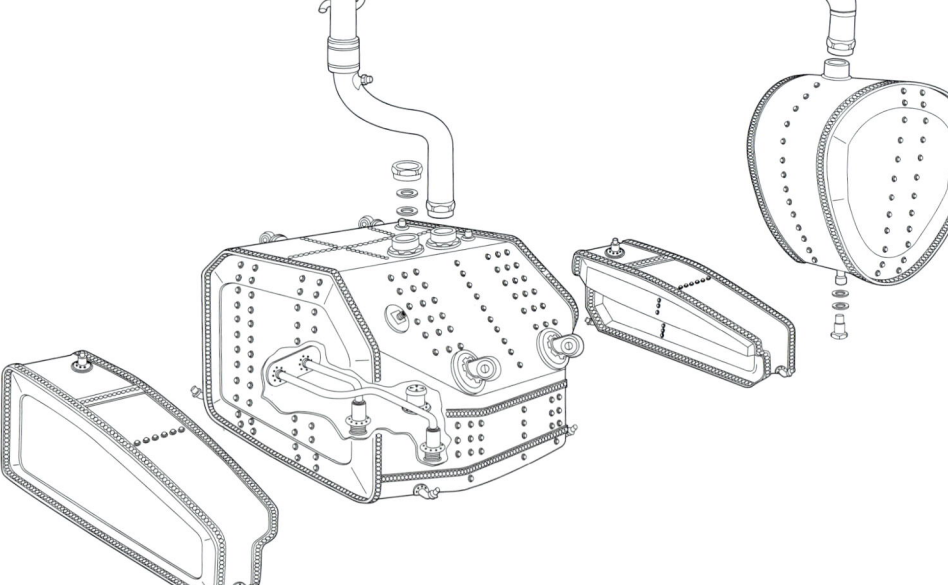

## I Gruppo ANR's Badges

### 1ª Squadriglia

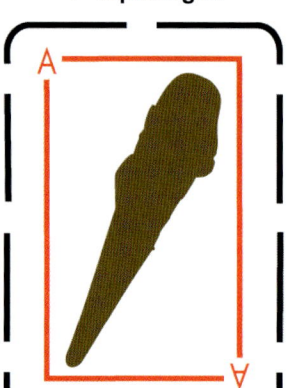

### 2ª Squadriglia

INCOCCA TENDE SCAGLIA

### 3ª Squadriglia

A small sprung panel situated on the port side of the fuselage provided access to a tri-pole socket that was used to control the electrical system without necessarily having to switch on all electrical units on board. The top left picture shows the panel in the closed position. The top right picture shows the panel in the open position.

From left to right are the refuelling cap for the supplementary tank, the dynamic socket, and the refuelling cap for the main tank. The dynamic socket provided pressure to all grouped air tubes and fitted close to the supplementary tank's refuelling cap.

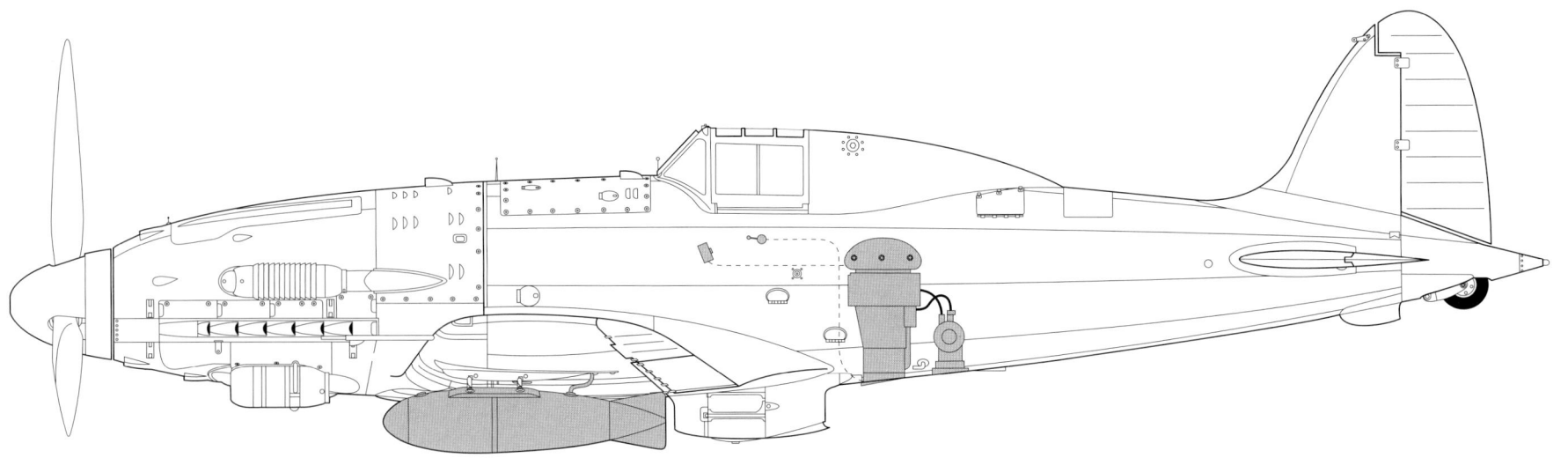

# Macchi C.205 recce I Series

Built in a dozen examples and modified from regular production, recce Veltros were all equipped with an original German Zeiss camera, placed behind the cockpit, and with 100- or 150-liter underwing fuel tanks.

# Macchi C.205 GA and S Version

These unofficial, long-range versions were field-realized in 1944 in Puglia to extend the C.205's range. III Series became GA by replacing the 12.7 mm machine guns with hand-made 200-liter fuel tanks. Due to the ineffective 7.7 mm wing armament, I Series planes were frequently fitted with underwing droppable fuel tanks while retaining the two cowl-mounted 12.7 mm guns.

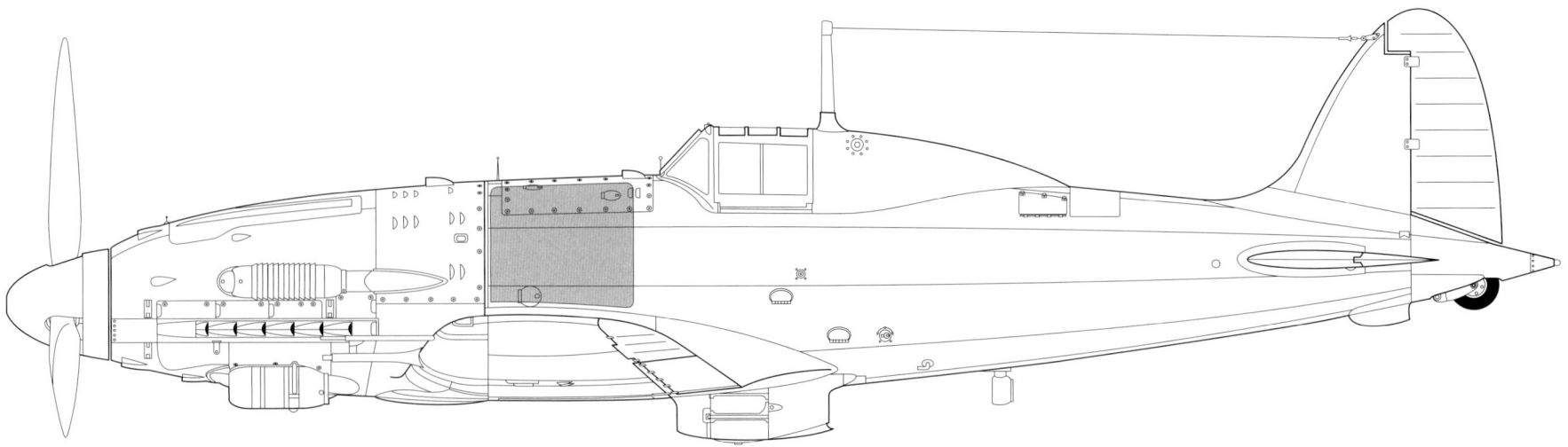

Some of the C.205s serving with the ANR were equipped with the standard German Revi C/12 gunsight. It is unknown whether these gunsights were fitted on the express request of German pilots when these aircraft were serving with JG/77, as happened with the inversion of throttle handle movement, or as a measure to standardize aircraft equipment with that of the German ally. (D'Amico e Valentini)

A genuine gunsight, but incorrect compass, O.M.I. type 2 were fitted to the Aermacchi C.205 during a ceremony in 1992.

This cockpit was often-photographed while it was still at the Macchi factory. The cockpit belongs to C.205, MM.9488, and is fitted with a San Giorgio Type B gunsight similar to what the C.200 and C.202 adopted. The compass is the O.M.I. 3 type. The fighter's serial number is engraved onto a tag fixed between the rudder pedals. Above the rudder pedals are four switches for the round counter to the fuselage-mounted 12.7 mm and wing-mounted 7.7 mm guns. These counters moved every five rounds until only 100 rounds were left. At that point, a red light came on and alerted the pilot about the low rounds.

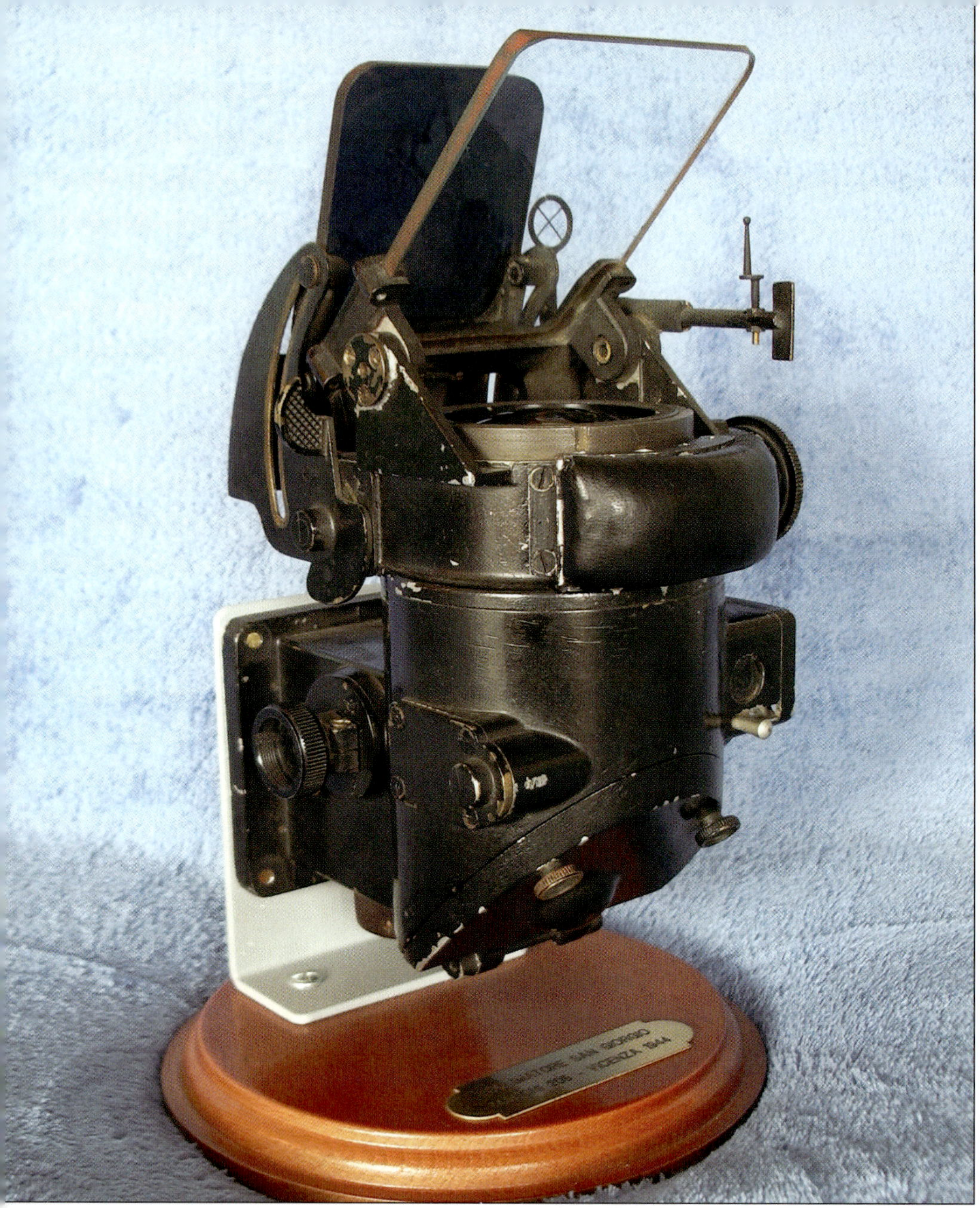

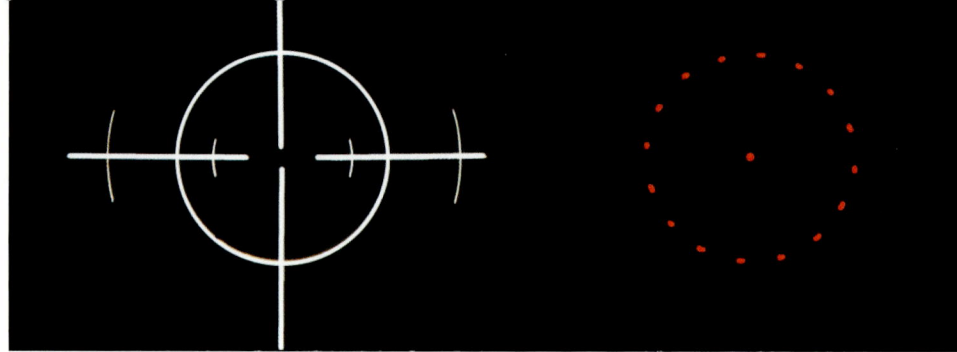

Through the switch handle positioned on the front, the pilot could choose between two different aiming cross-hair patterns, shown here. (Mauro Morsoletto)

(Above and Lower Right) This very rare and original San Giorgio Type C gunsight comes from an ANR C.205 and was standard fit on the III/VI Series C.205s. The San Giorgio Type C reflector gunsight, manufactured by San Giorgio in its La Spezia location, was appreciated for its precision and ease of use. Although the gunsight was provided with a deflection regulator, this item was rarely used since direct aiming through the opaque reflector glass was preferred. A sun screen was also available for the angled reflector glass to reduce glare. (Mauro Morsoletto)

52

The two types of cine-cameras used on Macchi C.205s were the Avia (left) and the Guidon-cine (right).

The Guidon-cine is loaded with its 120 meters of film.

With the Guidon-cine open, its outer cover and film magazine are visible.

The initial AVIA was flanked by the more reliable Guidon-cine, manufactured in Guidonia's Regia Aeronautica location. The Guidon-cine was smaller, lightweight, and faster to build.

## Photo-recce and Cine Veltros
### CINEAVIA equipped C.205s

- Two wing-mounted "Guidon-cine" or AVIA cine-cameras with 120 meters of film
- Normal I Series or III Series wing armament

## Camera equipped C. 205s

- One Zeiss RB. 50/30 planimetric camera and driving motor in fuselage
- No rear fuselage 80-liter fuel tank
- Two underwing racks
- Two underwing droppable 250-liter fuel tanks
- No radio equipment
- Normal I Series or III Series wing armament

Summer 1943—This I Series C.205, MM.9379, is assigned to the 351ª Squadriglia, 155° Gruppo, 51° Stormo in Sicily. The plane is fitted with a cine-camera. The CINEAVIA equipment is attached to the leading edge of the port wing, and the camera lens is covered by an aerodynamic fairing, together with the wing armament. The plane has the radio antenna typical of the later III Series. The rabbit painted on the nose is the pilot's personal emblem. Capitano Giovanni Franchini had the lowest-numbered aircraft in the unit, as seen from the "00" code. Franchini flew a very low-level photographic sortie with this plane over the U.S. Fleet during the Sicilian landings and suffered a certain amount of damage. He became a qualified test pilot after the war and was the first to fly above Mach 1 in an Aerfer Sagittario. (Franchini Family)

The first C.205 prototype, MM.9827 has just received its camouflage scheme. The oil radiators were left unpainted and in their original semi-curved shape. Under the left wing is a little cine-camera enclosed in a shaped cover. This device was probably used to record flying tests of the new machine. After the oil radiators were replaced, this plane became the prototype of the photo-recce Veltros. MM.9827 was lost on 9 December 1942, during a bombing raid over Turin. (Leoni via Brancaccio)

Macchi's external 150-liter fuel tank was equipped on a few C.202s and a number of C.205s. The tank's fuel cap is at the front. The overall color was probably Verde Oliva Scuro 2. Another smaller 100-liter fuel tank was available without its vertical fins. (Collection D'Amico and Valentini)

The cockpit interior of a C.205 fotografico (photo recce) is equipped with a Zeiss Rb. 50/30 fixed-focus camera placed in the rear fuselage behind the pilot's seat. In front of the control column is the OMI shutter control box. On the left is the selector with the rotating handle for aperture. (Udiente-Taliento)

Letter "C" marks the lever that controlled opening the sliding circular panel for the objective view, located behind the water radiator under the C.205 fotografico's belly.

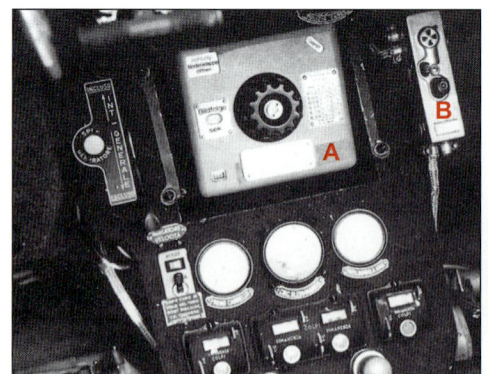

"A" indicates a German intervallometer, and "B" indicates the camera switch. (A.M.)

The port navigation light is fitted inside a framed, molded plexiglass that could easily be dismantled.

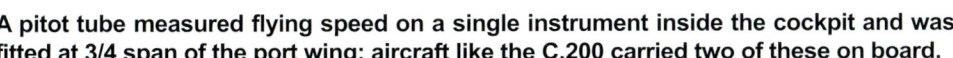

A pitot tube measured flying speed on a single instrument inside the cockpit and was fitted at 3/4 span of the port wing; aircraft like the C.200 carried two of these on board.

The starboard aileron of the C.205 consisted of a metal frame covered in *Makò Resistenza 2000* cotton fabric. As with all Macchi fighters, the C.205's starboard wing was 20 cm shorter in span to compensate for propeller torque.

The principle hinge on this Macchi C.205 aileron is surrounded by an oval screwed-on panel and covered by the classic rectangular thin sheet of Macchi design.

This example of a Macchi C.205 aileron hinge has a hole through which the crew could reach the fastening with a tube spanner.

This simpler Macchi C.205 aileron hinge has a single fairing that allowed movement.

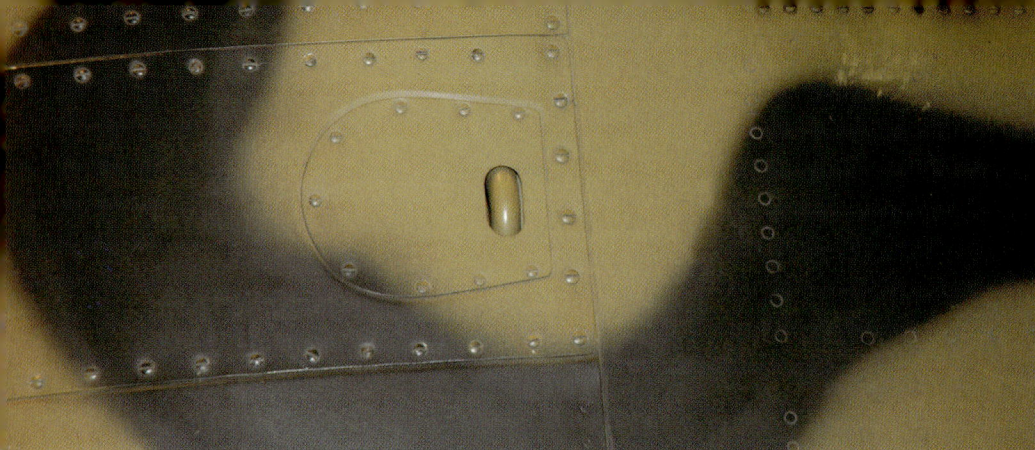

The small disc above the wing, aft of the 20 mm cannon, consisted of a visual undercarriage position signal—red when retracted, white when extended.

This wing skin surface shows the oval access panels to the armament box and the rectangular panel that covers the Mauser MG 151/20 cannon. Holes for fitting the underwing pylon can be seen, with screws across the whole wing section

The ominous mouth of the 20 mm Mauser cannon is clearly visible. Although generally referred to as a cannon, this weapon could better be classified as a heavy machine gun in regard to caliber and definition.

The twelve screws held the access panel (two per wing) in place. This panel allowed a crew member to reach the conical wing-to-fuselage mounting bolts.

The Mauser 20 mm cannon was installed in the wing of the Veltro. At its front is the expansion hub for its fitting, and at the rear end are the electrical wires for the cannon's feed and re-arm run. To the right side of the photo is the armament bay that feeds rounds directly into the gun's firing chamber.

The Veltro's oval panels to the armament bays were easily opened my making a half turn on the flat knob fixed at its center. This action turned three linchpins that opened the same panel. The armament belt was inserted into the three oval recesses in the wing skin. Inside the inner recess were a firing relay and electrical supply wires. Of great simplicity, the Mauser was armed and fired electrically.

This item is a 20 mm Mauser MG. 151/20 cannon perforation/incendiary round of the Panzerbrechend Brand. The Veltro carried 250 rounds per gun with a counter inside the cockpit that marked every single round fired, as opposed to the counter for the two SAFAT 12.7 mm guns. (V. Kertmorgant)

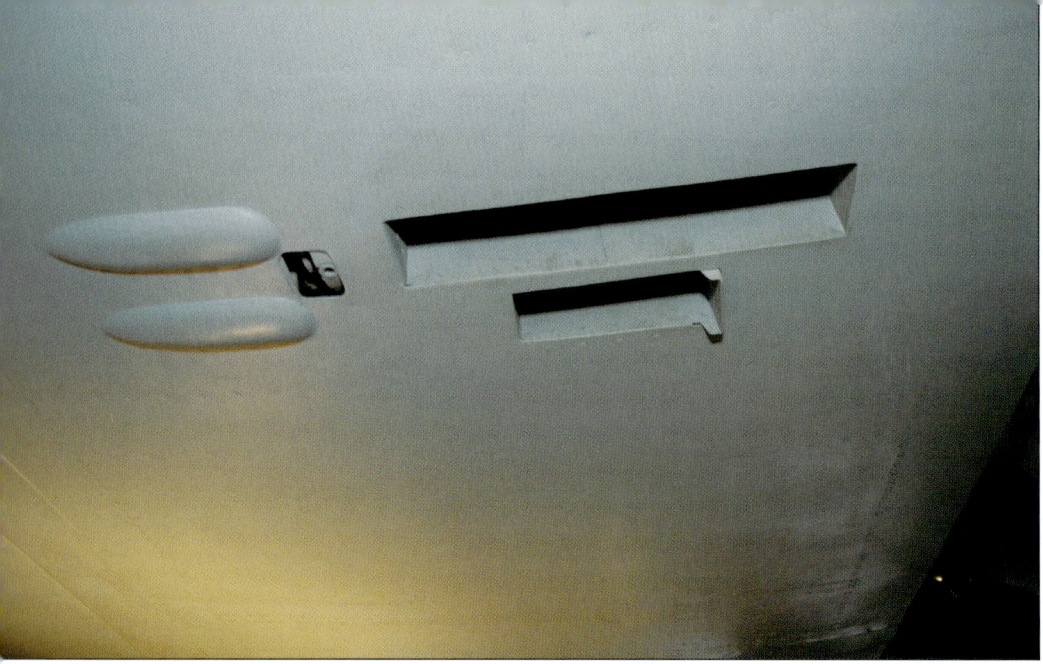

Spent rounds from the 20 mm were not recovered; they were ejected through a large opening below the Veltro's wings. Further inboard, a smaller outlet ejected the cartridge links, which were similarly discarded. The links were provided with a small metal sheet that kept the links away from the wing skin surface.

Aft of these two outlets was a horizontal hole that allowed hot, firing gases to escape. The two large fairings housed the cannon rearmament mechanism.

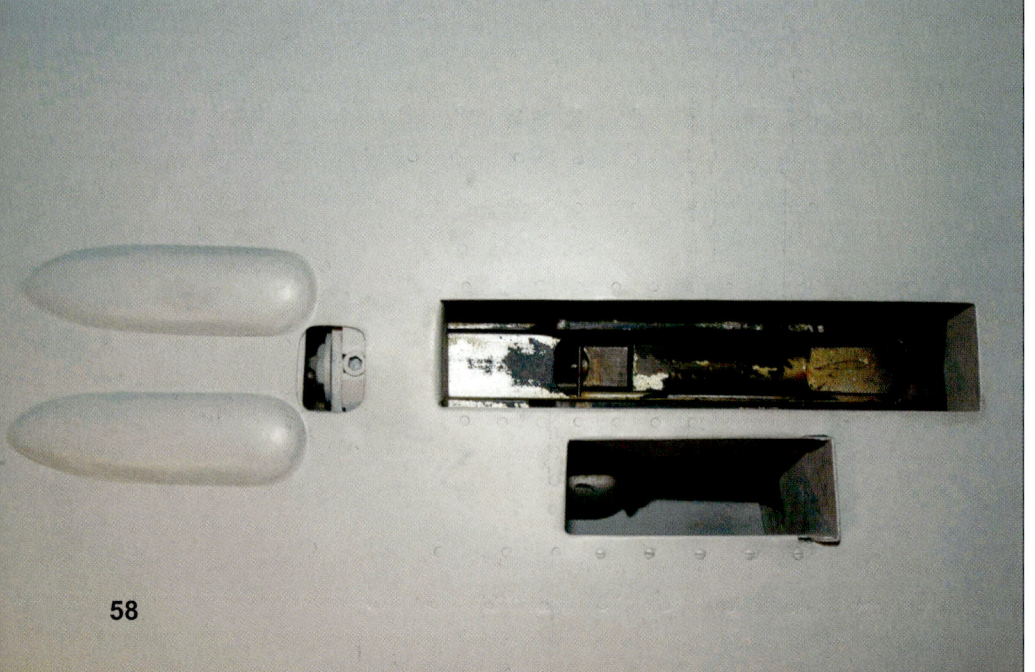

The 20 mm Mauser cannon is housed inside the wing armament bay in the Veltro's wing. This area was accessible through a wide, rectangular door that slid backward after six securing screws were removed. Ease of maintenance was guaranteed, and the entire cannon could be removed if necessary.

(Top) In addition to the wing cannon and fuselage-mounted SAFAT guns, this aircraft is fitted with underwing racks that were originally designed to carry small/medium bombs but were transformed to carry supplementary 150-liter fuel tanks. Official Macchi documentation calls these racks *Travetti Benzina* (fuel pylons), which could carry up to 160 kilograms. (De Marchi)

(Bottom Left) The menacing cannon mouth shows its ribbed interior and forward centering ring. Initial velocity of the MG.151/20's shell was 790 meters per second with a rate of fire of 780 rounds per minute. Firing range was 850 meters.

(Bottom Right) 1940—Journalists at Venegono inspect a C.205 that was just overhauled for delivery to Egypt. Of 62 C.205s Egypt ordered, only 42 were actually delivered. Apart from the tall antenna and fixed tail wheel, the aircraft is up to the III Series standard. Whenever possible, the fixed tail wheel was adopted to simplify the aircraft's use. (AleniaAermacchi)

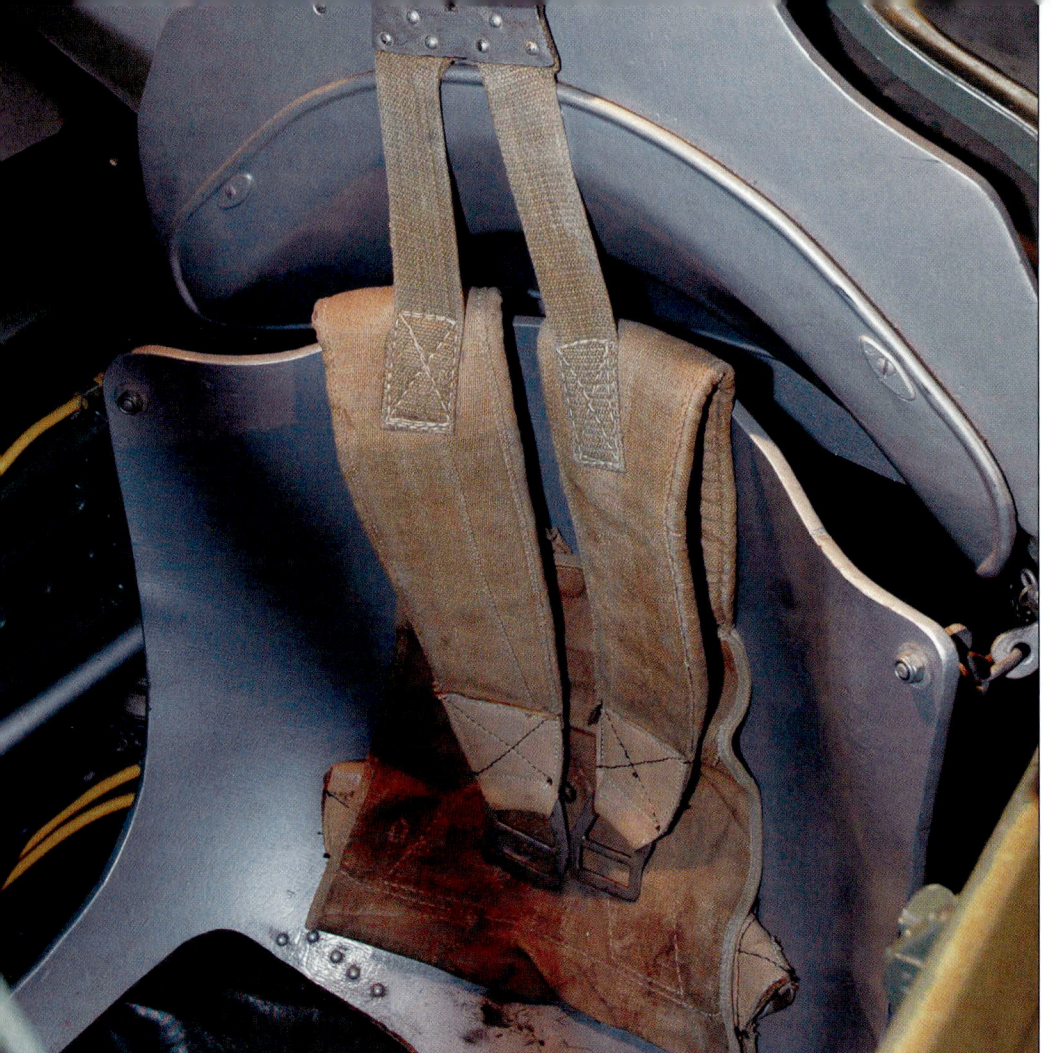

**(Seat Photos)** Harnesses on Italian aircraft were fixed at three points. The two buckles at the end of the straps clipped into a central metal buckle, which was fitted to a chain that ran between the pilot's legs. The harness was then tensioned inside the fairing behind the pilot's head by a metal cable that passed through the armored plate.

**(Knob Photo)** The wheel brake button was positioned on top of the C.202-type control column that was fitted on I Series C.205s. The weapons' trigger, lying along the grip, was positioned in front of the pilot and would not function when it was in safety mode. Upon turning the upper knob, the pilot could select "D" to fire the starboard gun, "S" to fire the port nose gun, or "TUTTE" (all) to fire all four weapons. During the "D" or "S" selection, the firing button raised the flow of compressed air to the guns so they could fire, moving clockwise. During the "TUTTE" selection, the firing button was located forward in regard to the pilot's index finger. A pair of round levers fitted to the sides of the cockpit operated the safety for the two SAFAT 7.7 mm guns

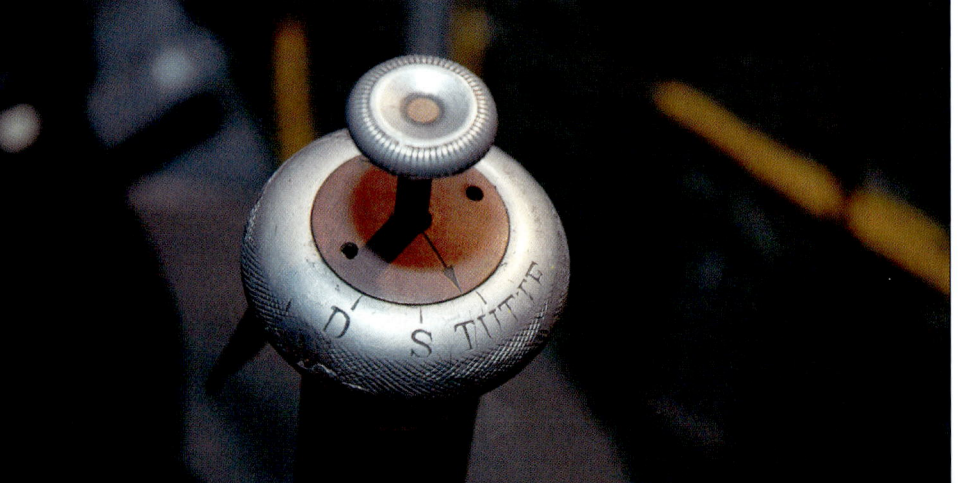

The folding canopy opened by pulling back a knobbed lever on the left of the frame that operated an internal spring to release the two securing pins and allowed the canopy to hinge open to starboard. Pulling both levers released the whole canopy. The side front glass panels slid backwards. The armored plate located behind the pilot's head was composed of 5 mm thick steel.

This compass is an original O.M.I. type 3, the standard for WWII Italian fighters.

Several original items are missing from the Venegono Veltro's cockpit. Missing items from MM.92166 include the fuselage guns rearming levers, the round counters, the oxygen nozzle, and parts of the starting panel.

During the second half of the 1980s, when this Veltro arrived at Venegono, initial hopes were to bring the plane back to flying condition, and items such as piping and instruments were removed to make way for a more modern installation.

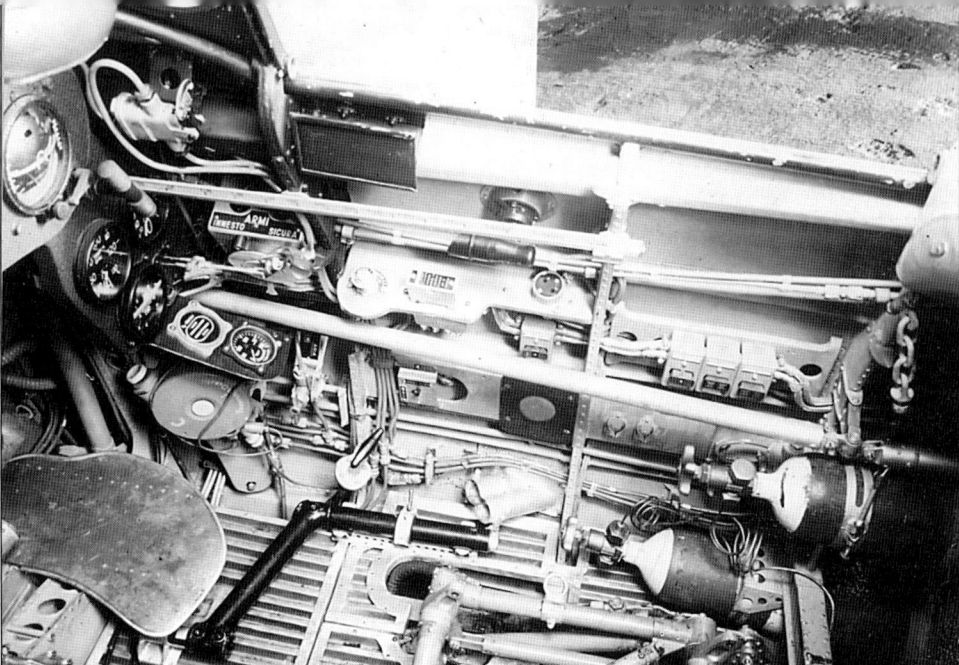

The small, molded panel, starboard of the cabin, houses the starting injector, the starting button, and a socket for the pilot's electrically warmed flying suit.

At port is the radio panel above the throttle together with the tailplane's trimming wheel. Internally, the cockpit is painted in anti-corrosion green except for the floor, armored plates, and seat, which are all painted silver. The inside face of the cockpit canopy frame was always matt black. (AleniaAermacchi)

This forward view is the cockpit of a four-gun I Series C.205. Note the C.202 type control column with the starting handle fitted to the floor at starboard, the German Dräger Auer II° type oxygen nozzle, and the arming discs of the two wing guns.

(Above) A series of thermal switches can be seen on the starboard sidewall of the cockpit. These switches do not form part of the C.205's standard equipment and were probably installed for experimental purposes. (AleniaAermacchi)

(Right) This forward view shows a III Series fighter and its cockpit. Visible is the definitive type of control column featuring a bomb release button, protected by a small lever. Apart from serving as a safety catch, this lever became the firing trigger for the fuselage and wing guns. To the bomb release button's right is the mushroom brake actuator. (AleniaAermacchi)

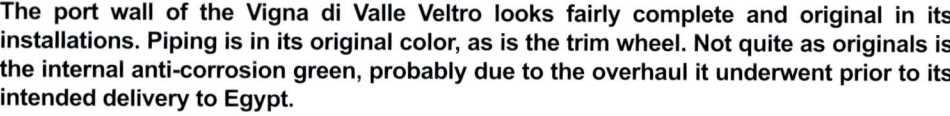

The port wall of the Vigna di Valle Veltro looks fairly complete and original in its installations. Piping is in its original color, as is the trim wheel. Not quite as originals is the internal anti-corrosion green, probably due to the overhaul it underwent prior to its intended delivery to Egypt.

The water radiator flap lever was fixed to a support on the left-hand side, together with the Corbetta filter butterfly valve, and the undercarriage oil pressure drain. Above, this lever secured the pilot's shoulder straps.

The Vigna di Valle Veltro's starboard sidewall shows the silver rudder bar, oxygen nozzle, and graduated fuel gauge. This instrument was the only one onboard that indicated fuel level, an empirical but efficient system.

The German Dräger Auer II° oxygen device was fitted with two control instruments. The upper instrument was a visible aid whose white blades moved with the pilot's rate of breathing. The lower instrument was a pressure indicator. Below these devices is the tap that controlled compressed air flow to the guns.

The control panel on the Venegono example was rebuilt with the aim of bringing the aircraft to flying condition. Nearly all the engine instruments have been substituted with modern equivalents while the round-counter, compass, and oxygen nozzle have been removed. A plastic gunsight replica was installed. Notwithstanding all of these replacements, the fighter retains the charm of an operational machine, probably due to the fact that MM.92166 participated in a number of aerial battles and shot down a couple of Allied aircraft.

Easily accessible on the right-hand side of the panel was the command for switching fuselage guns to live. The lever was operated to arm or disarm the synchronized transmissions found on the pair of SAFAT 12.7 mm guns.

The throttle consisted of two levers with a button on top. The longer lever with the red button consists of the Nassetti type fuel throttle that was pulled backwards to increase engine power. In case of emergency or when taking off at full load, a power boost was available for a short while by pressing the button that allowed the lever to move further back. This type of boost was known as +100. Next to this lever was the one that controlled the propeller pitch. This lever could be moved manually or set to a predetermined position by simply pressing the button on top. On all surviving Veltros, the throttle group has been modified to operate the other way around.

Starting commands for the engine were positioned on the small panel on the right. Two electric control boxes and the navigation light switch are positioned below.

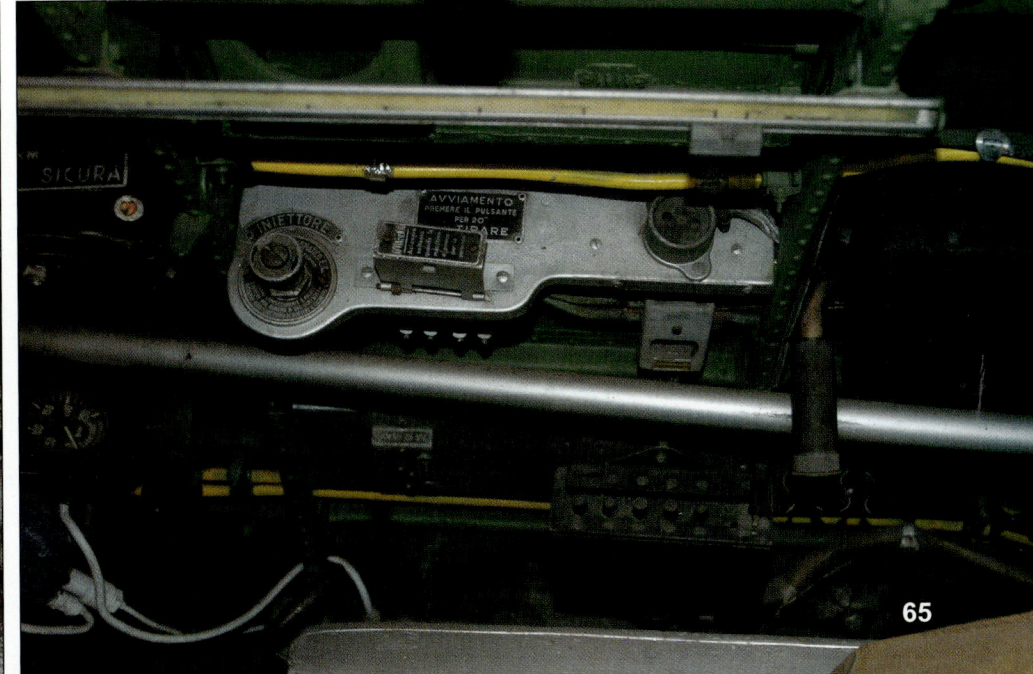

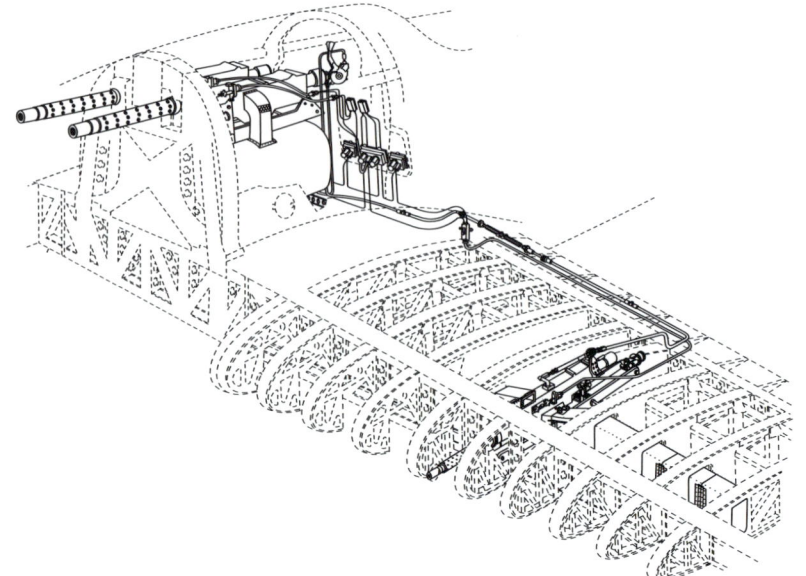

This recreated maintenance manual drawing is for the I Series wing-mounted 7.7 SAFAT machine guns. The ammunition link feed is supplied by a simple rectangular box.

Summer 1943—The pet dog of 352ª Squadriglia rests on the wing, with a 7.7 mm wing machine gun, of a C.205 I Series Veltro at Capoterra (Sardinia). (D'Amico and Valentini)

The nose armament of I Series Veltros is illustrated in this recreated drawing from the aircraft's manual. The two synchronization push-rods are fitted in the upper front part of the engine. The two cocking handles, the ammo counters, and the synchronization switch (on the right side) are on the instrument panel.

This recreated drawing shows the installation of the nose machine guns for the C.205. The barrels' cooling tubes are visible together with the MG's fixing mounts. The ammunition boxes are in the middle, and the spent cartridges container is on the outer part of the installation.

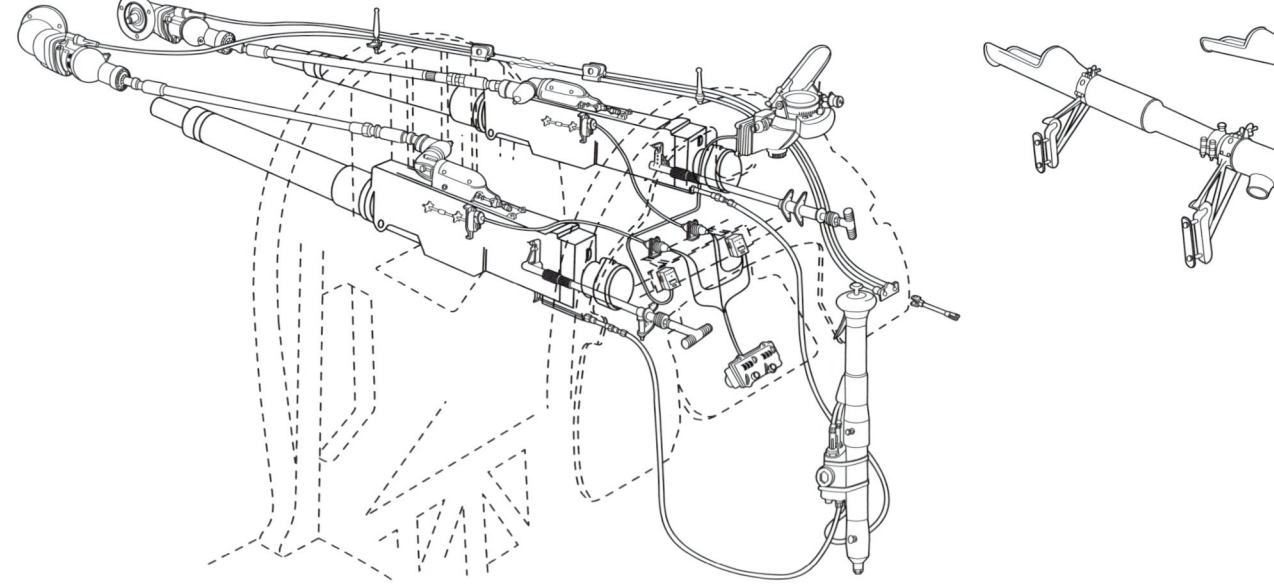

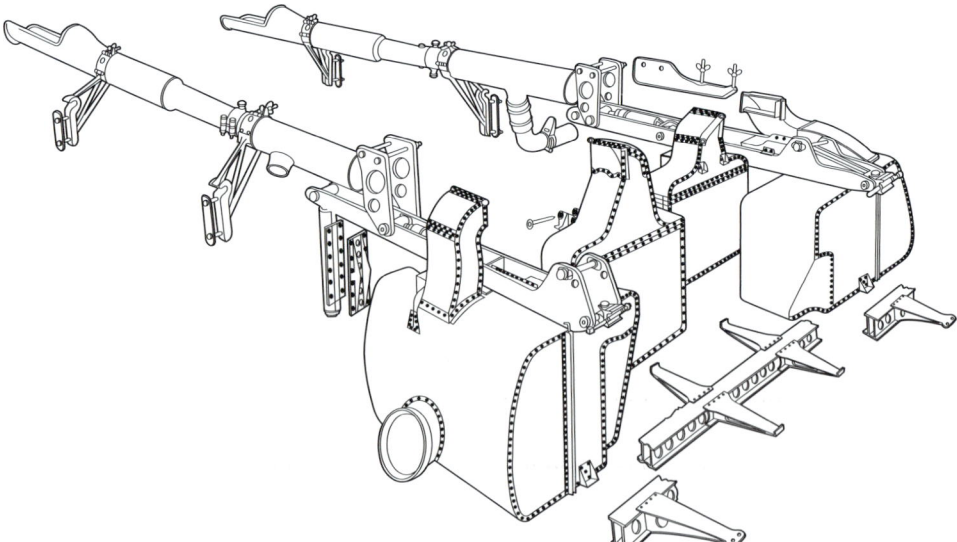

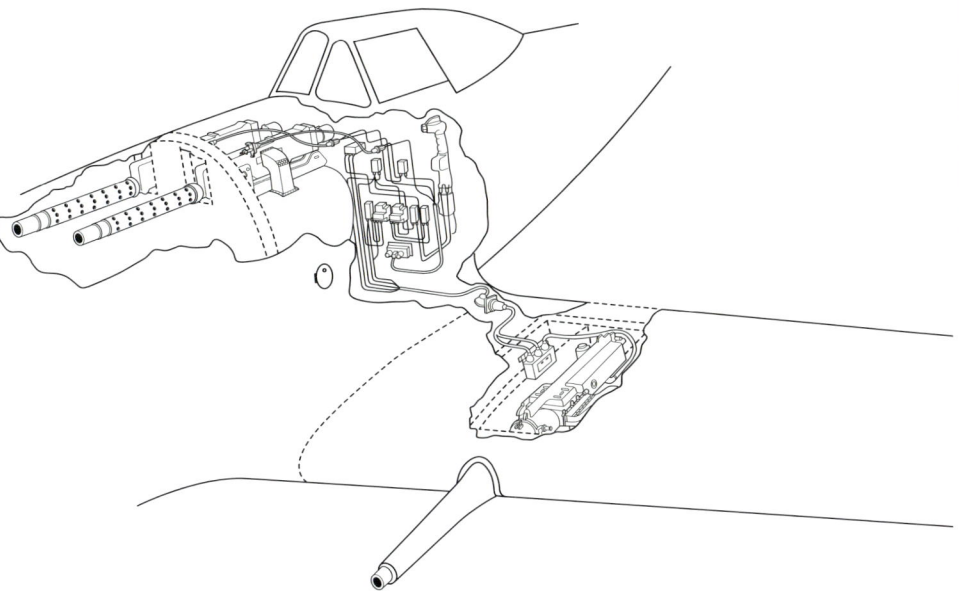

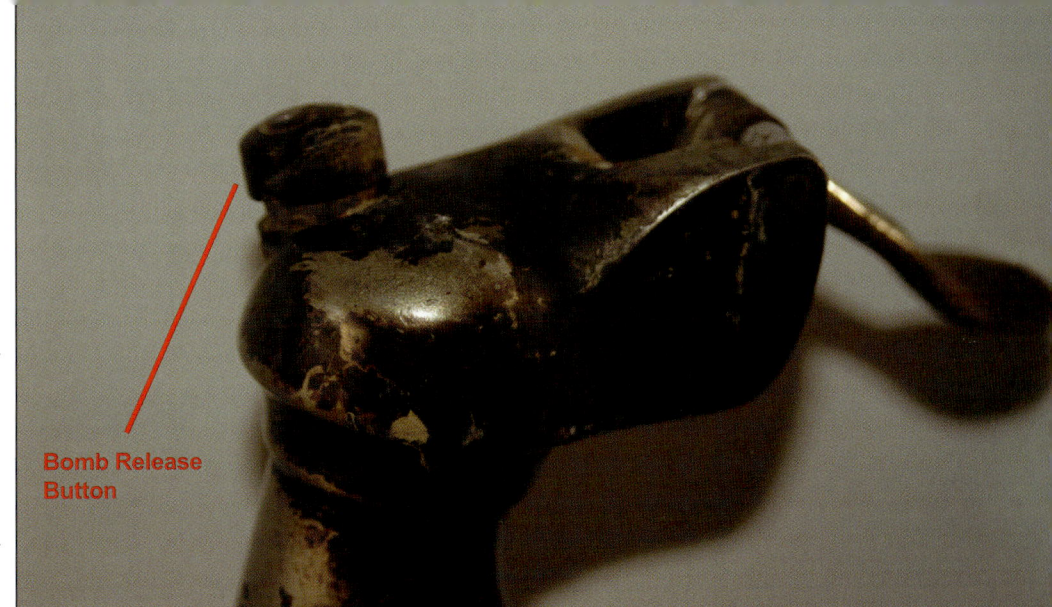

Bomb Release Button

The wing-mounted, electrically operated 20 mm Mauser cannon on the III Series was an effective and easy-to-use weapon, especially when compared to the nose-mounted MGs that were operated by compressed air.

Oxygen for high altitude was provided through a German Dräger Auer II° system that included two three-liter bottles (controlled by a regulator on the right-side of the cabin), a fluxmeter, a pressure gauge, and an oxygen mask.

The brake actuator is normally situated on top of the pilot's stick handle but is missing here.

The Macchi III Series pilot's control column has the small, hinged trigger button on the top. When tilting the lever downward, the pilot could depress the trigger button midway to fire the 12.7 mm nose guns only, or he could press the button fully to fire both MGs and the cannon. The recreated illustration next to the pilot's control column shows the complete pilot's stick with fast-type firing triggers.

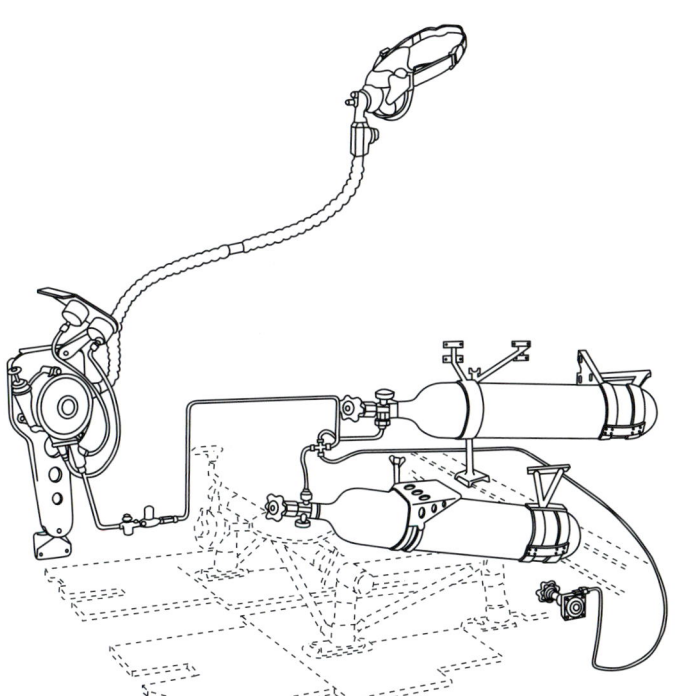

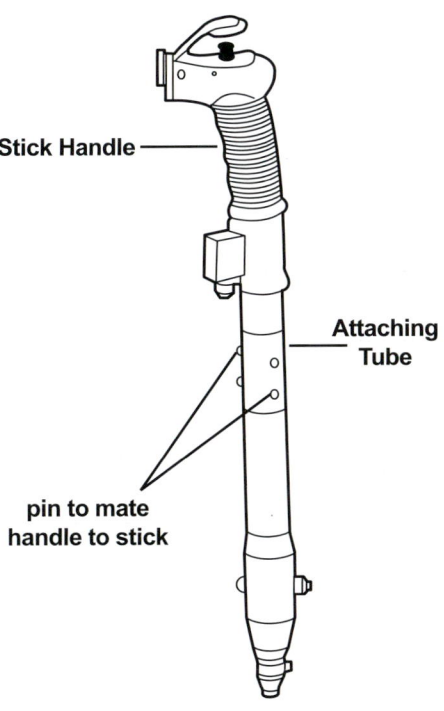

Stick Handle

Attaching Tube

pin to mate handle to stick

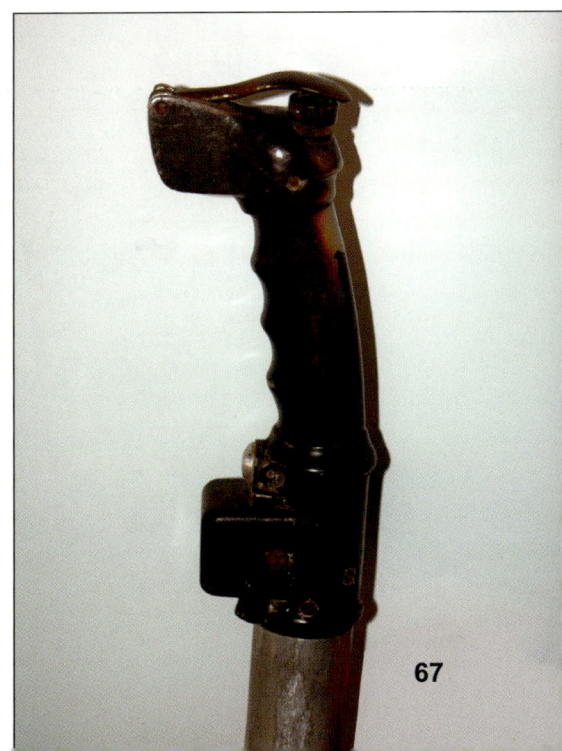

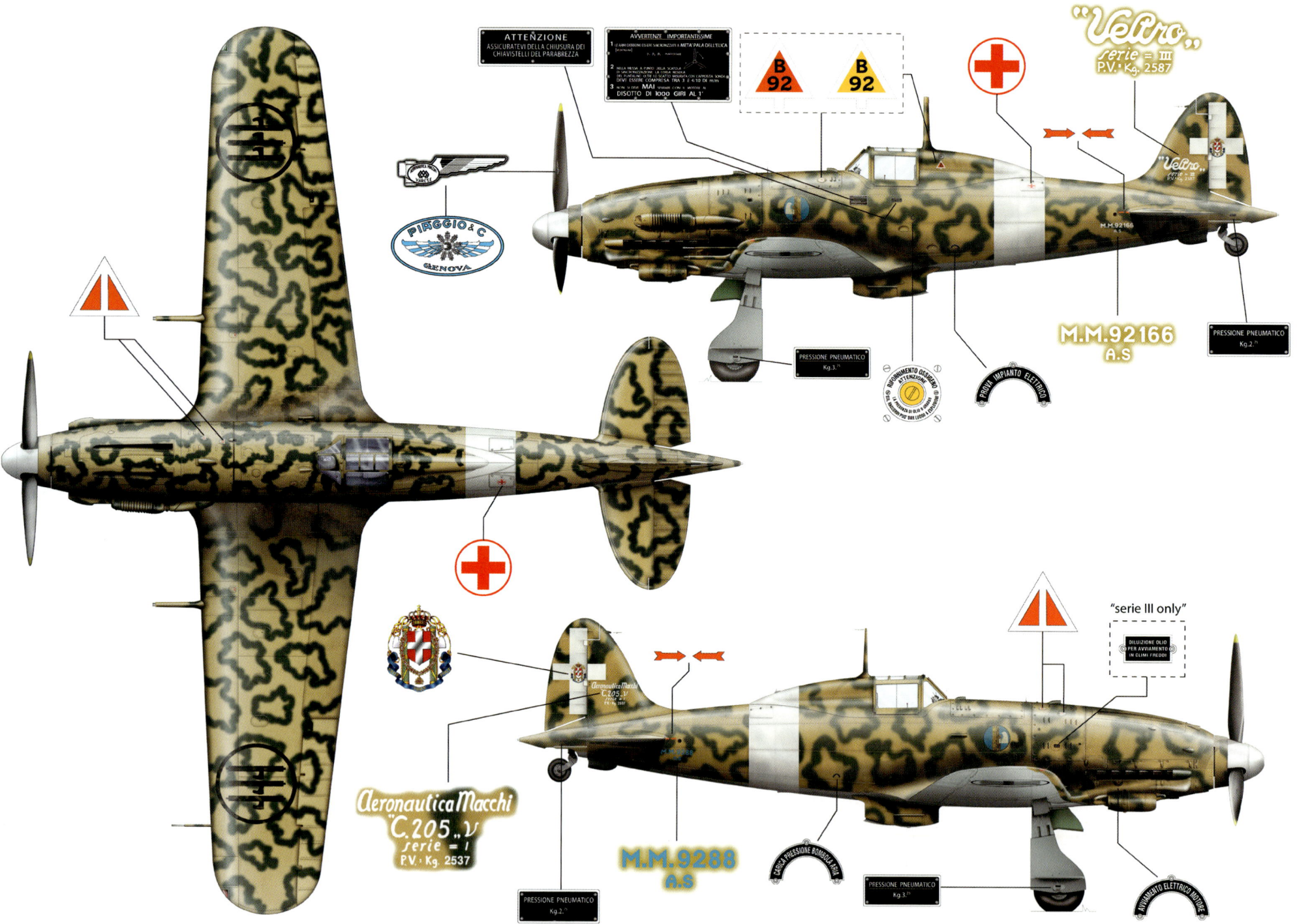

ATTENZIONE
ASSICURATEVI DELLA CHIUSURA DEI
CHIAVISTELLI DEL PARABREZZA

AVVERTENZE IMPORTANTISSIME

B 92

B 92

"Veltro"
serie = III
P.V.: Kg. 2587

PIAGGIO & C
GENOVA

PRESSIONE PNEUMATICO
Kg.3.¹ʼ

PRESSIONE PNEUMATICO
Kg.2.¹ʼ

M.M.92166
A.S

PROVA IMPIANTO ELETTRICO

"serie III only"

DILUIZIONE OLIO
PER AVVIAMENTO
IN CLIMI FREDDI

Aeronautica Macchi
C.205 "V
serie = I
P.V.: Kg. 2537

M.M.9288
A.S

CARICA PRESSIONE BOMBOLA AGILA

PRESSIONE PNEUMATICO
Kg.3.¹ʼ

AVVIAMENTO ELETTRICO MOTORE

PRESSIONE PNEUMATICO
Kg.2.¹ʼ

| NOCCIOLA CHIARO 4 | VERDE OLIVA SCURO 2 | VERDE ANTI CORROSIONE | GRIGIO AZZ. CHIARO 1 | RLM 74 | RLM 75 | RLM 76 | GIALLO CROMO 7 | BIANCO NEVE | AZZURRO 11 |
|---|---|---|---|---|---|---|---|---|---|
| FSC 30219 | FSC 34052 | FSC 34558 | FSC 36307 | FSC 34086 | FSC 36122 | FSC 36473 | FSC 23655 | FSC 37925 | FSC 35095 |

The *Riforma Mimetica* (camouflage reform) of 1942 standardized colors used on Italian aircraft. This standardization was mainly based on the these illustrated colors, which were defined through a series of color chips displayed on the well-known Table 10. With the continuation of the war in the North, aircraft that served with the ANR were repainted with the adopted colors and schemes of German inspiration, which resulted in highly marked variations.

In 1997, the Italian Air Force commemorated its 75th anniversary with a display of historic aircraft that included the Venengono C.205, MM.92166. The planes were marshaled out in the open country where they once went to war. Today, this C.205 is preserved and housed within the Macchi establishment, where it was built in June, 1943. (Paolo Francois)

MM.9287 was the first prototype of the Veltro in the prescribed Verde Oliva Scuro 2 finish and lacked tropical installations such as the Corbetta sand filter.

The second prototype, MM.9288, sits in front of the Guidonia hangars. The plane already has a serial number of a C.205 but appears to be painted in Azzurro 11. (A.M.)

Sottotenente Galbusera poses on Veltro I Series coded 84-3 at Galatina di Lecce just after the Armistice. The white fuselage band and the rudder cross have been sprayed over in Nocciola Chiaro 4 to increase camouflage while on the ground. (Galbusera)

Palermo-Boccadifalco airport, 1942—This I Series C.205 has just been delivered to the 1° Stormo though the plane does not carry the Stormo's code. However, the plane does carry the Archer insignia.

Summer 1943—Sottotenente Franchetti poses with C.205, MM.92204, number 4 of 91ª Squadriglia, 10° Gruppo, 4° Stormo at Castrovillari. (Galbusera via Brancaccio)

A C.205 from the 95 Squadriglia (18° Gruppo, 3° Stormo) takes off from Cerveteri. This unit participated in defending Rome. The unit operated a mixed squadron of C.202s, C.205s, and Me 109Gs. (A.M.)

Maresciallo Ennio Tarantola poses in front of his C.205 III Series, in which he fought an epic battle over the southern coast of Sardinia on 2 August 1943. (Tarantola)

Cineavia C.205, MM.9377, now CV-V, is under Australian control, and the ground crew has just over-painted the RA insignia with their own. Apart from the two cine-cameras, CV-V is also fitted with a DF loop antenna under the fuselage. (A. Thomas via Phil Butler)

This prototype is in its original configuration with the half-buried barrel type oil radiators and non-tropicalized compressor air intake. The plane displays its new serial number, MM.9287, on the tail. The Venturi tube is in its original ventral position ahead of the radiator on an aircraft that retains very few characteristics of the Folgore from which it was derived, together with the unbalanced elevators. The plane was later transferred to Guidonia to complete its flight evaluation and tests while full production of the I Series was well underway.

C.205 Series 81-1, MM.9360, belonged to the 81ª Squadriglia (6° Gruppo, 1° Stormo) that was operational in Sicily in mid-February 1943. During the spring, this unit frequently faced the British Spitfires over the Sicilian channel and recorded a number of victories. This plane was probably assigned to the Squadriglia commander and survived the Armistice to continue flying through the war of Liberation against the Germans in the Balkans following an extensive overhaul. The plane is fitted with the early type radio antenna with the aerial consisting of three elements that meet a dipole entry above the rear cockpit fairing.

The 4° Stormo Caccia was based at Castrovillari, during the summer of 1943, to oppose the heavy Allied attacks on Sicily and Calabria. I Series C.205s that were in service were supplemented by a number of new C.205 III Series such as 91-4, MM.92204, taken on charge on 6 September 1943, and immediately thrown into battle. The lack of the Rampant Horse and a hyphen to separate the code numbers and the improperly finished number 9 serve to illustrate with what haste aircraft were being pressed into service. The 91-4 remained operational throughout the Co-Belligerent war and retired from service in the 1950s.

Following the Sicilian landings of July 1943, the No. 3 Squadron Royal Australian Air Force captured this I Series Macchi C.205, MM.9377. Coming from the 4°Stormo, this example was one of the few Veltros built and delivered to the Regia Aeronautica fitted with cine-camera equipment that consisted of two AVIA units in the wings. The No. 3 Squadron personnel often flew this Veltro for evaluation and for fun, especially by Flg. Off. Arthur Dawkings, who formed a positive impression of the aircraft. This I Series aircraft is fitted with the III Series antenna.

Capitano Morino, CO of 151ª Squadriglia, 20° Gruppo of 51° Stormo at Milis, Sardinia, flew MM.92170 during the summer of 1943. *Padella* (pan) was painted on the nose as a joke to the officer. Photographed shortly after the Armistice, this C.205 shows the overpainting of its fascist markings. (Coll. R. Baseler via D. Mocabee—A. Ragatzu)

Castrovillari in Calabria, summer 1943—Sottotenente Galbusera stands next to a C.205 III Series 90-2, MM.92163. Overspray of the white fuselage band and the Savoy cross has taken the place of the Rampant Horse. (Galbusera)

This Veltro's left wing bears a large, mottled camouflage. (IX° Gruppo CIO via Brancaccio)

An ANR crewman poses in C.205 6-2, MM.92277, flown by Sottotenente Lugari. The pilot's initials have been painted on the humped fairing aft of the cockpit. (CMPR)

September 1943—Tenente Mario Mazzoleni and his Veltro, coded 378-6, posed for the camera before they reached Puglie from Sardinia. A small, yellow chevron was added below the canopy, and the camouflage scheme was retouched. (Mazzoleni)

Three ground crew members rest on a III Series Veltro belonging to the 2ª Squadriglia (1° Gruppo) ANR. The aircraft is finished in typical German colors with the lower section of the engine cowling painted yellow. (CMPR)

Sottotenente Lugari of the 2ª Squadriglia, 1° Gruppo ANR boards his C.205. He was killed in action on 6 April 1944 on the Austrian border and was credited with victory over two P-38s and one B-24. (CMPR)

Maresciallo Magnaghi, a highly experienced pilot who passed away after suffering leg injuries during combat on 11 May 1944, converses with Sergente Maggiore Svanini and Laiolo.

This Veltro 23-1, MM.92302, was the last of the III Series to be built and was assigned to the 1ᵃ Squadriglia (1° Gruppo Caccia) ANR. Maresciallo Gorrini, decorated with the Gold Medal for Military Valor, often flew this aircraft in combat and was credited with 19 individual victories. This fighter survived the war and was overhauled by Macchi. Later, the plane served with the 3° Gruppo Scuole (training group), Lecce, toward the end of 1947. The white fuselage band and yellow lower part of the engine cowling consisted of markings introduced in April 1944.

This C.205 (serial number is unknown) is unusually decorated and belongs to the 351ᵃ Squadriglia (20° Gruppo, 51° Stormo) based at Cagliari-Elmas airfield in Sardinia during summer 1943. After the Armistice and before the unit's definitive transfer to Puglia, the aircraft received new tricolor markings that were added over the previous ones. The unit painters used red for the Veltro logo and individual code number 1—the same color they used to paint the spinner front and tail cone.

On 4 March 1944, Capitano Trevisini was assigned to deliver this C.205 to the Squadrigilia Bonet at Turin, but he defected and landed at Lausanne. Both the pilot and the damaged fighter were interned. The aircraft was repaired, test flown by Swiss pilots, given back to Italy on 24 June 1947, and piloted by Maggiore Spadaccini. This profile show the C.205's new roundels over its wartime markings. Following a period of service with the 5° Stormo, the aircraft was relegated to training duties until withdrawn in the mid-1950s.

The Royal Egyptian Air Force received two different batches of Macchi C.205 fighters, the majority made up of C.202 conversions. Number 1214 formed part of the first lot of 24 examples that received RAF-type camouflage and remained in service up to the end of the 1940s. The serial number is indicated in Arabic characters on the white fuselage band.

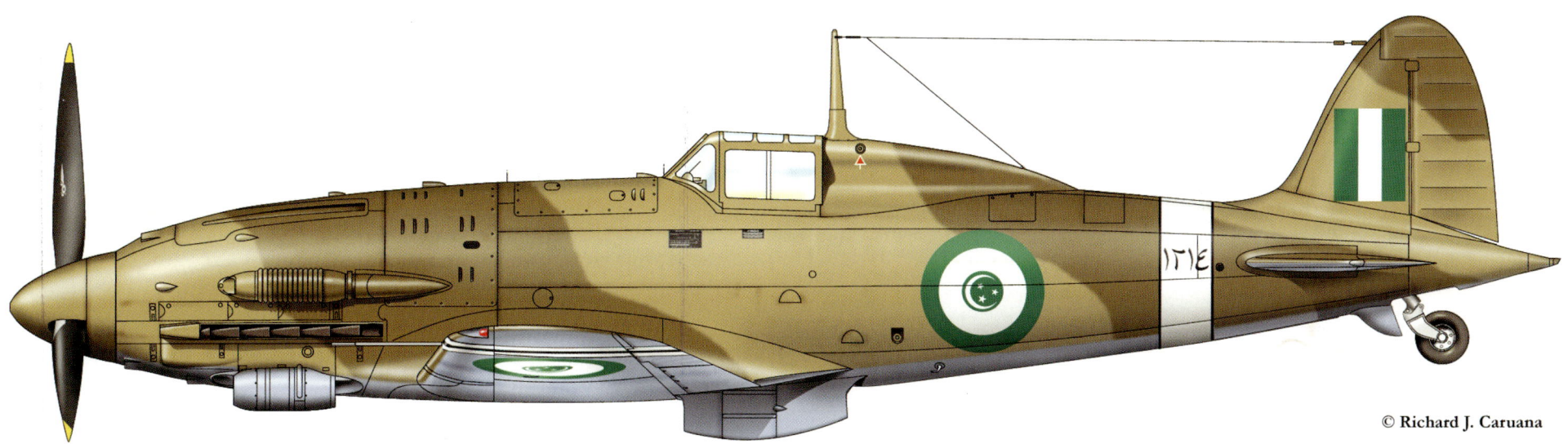

© Richard J. Caruana

A number of C.205 fuselages were abandoned in the grass after the end of WWII. MM.98277 was the 10th VI Series Veltro produced and flown between March and April 1944. (D'Amico And Valentini)

MM.9695, coded 21-5, was a C.202 XI Series that served with the 4° Stormo in Sicily when coded 91-7. When converted to a C.205, this plane served with the 21° Gruppo. The fixed tail wheel and supplementary 150-liter fuel tanks where produced by Macchi. (D'Amico and Valentini)

Reggio Emilia, 1944—This VI Series C.205 carries a wavy band color scheme. Of approximately 15 produced, 10 C.205s are confirmed as having served with the Squadriglia Autonoma M. Fusco-Bonet and the I° Gruppo Caccia. (D'Amico and Valentini)

A serviceman poses in front of a well-worn I Series C.205. The aircraft served with the 51° Stormo in southern Italy during the Co-Belligerent period. (Luigi Iacomino)

A reconditioned C.205 was being prepared for Egyptian export. The uniform delivery scheme was unofficially named *petrol green*. (AleniaAermacchi)

On return to Italy from Swiss internment, MM.92289 had it its spiral on the spinner and all ANR markings removed. A black 74 was added below the wings and on its fuselage sides. (Giorgio Ferrari Via Pierluigi Castellani)

After WWII, numerous C.200, C.202, and C.205 airframes were found in the Macchi hangar. The airframes carried German, ANR, and Co-Belligerent markings. Some of these frames were reconditioned for the Italian Air Force, and some other air frames were sold to Egypt.

All post-war Italian Air Force aircraft were finished with an aluminum scheme like the one worn by this I Series Veltro, MM.9305. Alphanumeric codes in British RAF style are painted below the wings. (Giorgio Ferrari via Pierluigi Castellani)

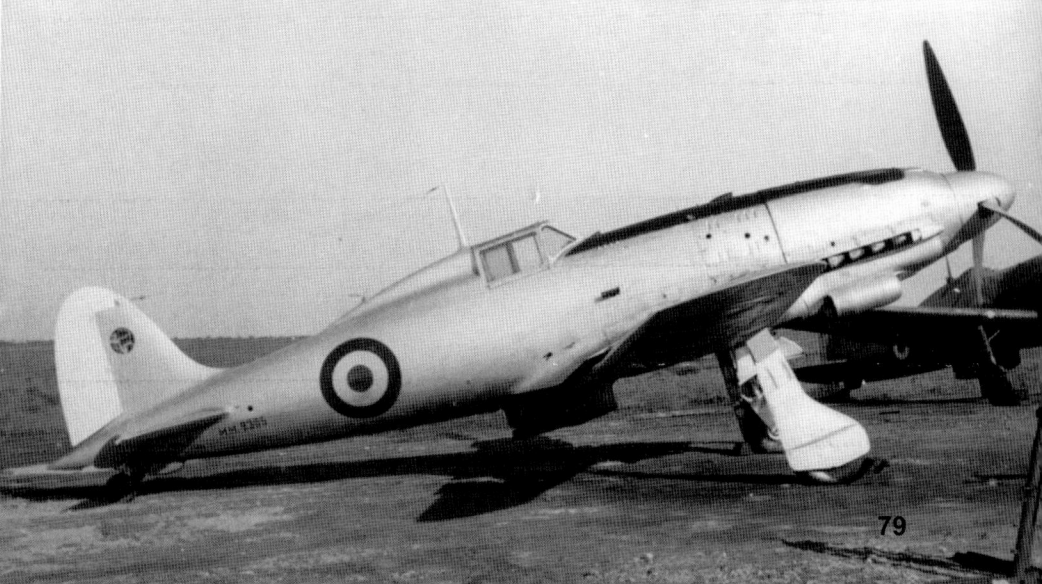

This C.205 is now preserved at the Vigna di Valle Museum. Here, the plane appears in its original aluminum finish during its stay at the Palazzo Vela at Turin toward the end of the 1960s. Most of the aircraft earmarked for the future Museo Storico of Vigna di Valle where kept here at that time (A.M.)

This C.205, MM.9305, was one of the few lucky planes that ended its operational career with the Italian Air Force during peacetime. This I Series Veltro served with the 1° and 4° Stormo of the Regia Aeronautica as well as the 51° Stormo Co-Belligerent Air Force. After the war, the plane was painted silver with a black anti-dazzle panel and carried the insignia of Diana the Hunter of the 5° Stormo while flying from Orio al Serio, Bergamo, at the end of the 1940s. Below the wing, the plane wore the individual code V-33 in black.